MW00467099

TROPICAL FRUIT RECIPES
Rare and Exotic Fruits

RARE FRUIT COUNCIL INTERNATIONAL, INC.
MIAMI, FLORIDA

Copyright © 1981 by
Rare Fruit Council International, Inc.
3280 South Miami Avenue, Miami, Florida 33129

No part of this book may be reproduced or utilized
in any form without permission in writing from the
publisher except by a reviewer who wishes to quote
brief passages for the purpose of a review.

Manufactured in the United States of America

ISBN 0-916224-71-6
Distributed by Banyan Books, Inc.
P.O. Box 1160, Miami, Florida 33143

Foreword

The Rare Fruit Council International, founded in 1955, was organized to promote the development and use of tropical fruits in South Florida. The benign climate is conducive to growing many tropical fruits that cannot be fruited in any other area of the continental United States. The objectives of the Rare Fruit Council include obtaining superior varieties of tropical fruits from other countries, selecting meritorious seedlings found in the local area, and teaching members as well as the general public methods of propagation and the cultural requirements of fruit trees. In order to service these aims the members gather seeds, scions, and plants on trips to other countries, and they also exchange plant materials with foreign collaborators. Annual plant sales are held so that new species and varieties can be made available to the general public. In addition, interested groups in communities outside the Miami area have been assisted to form chapters, and several chapters have been started in other countries.

The first edition of *Tropical Fruit Recipes* was published in 1976. It was out of print within three years. Therefore, a committee composed of E. D. Ackerman, Carolyn Welch Betts, and Charles E. and Dorothy D. Vanderpool was designated to prepare a new edition. This committee is grateful to all contributors whose efforts made the first edition a success, and also to those who helped prepare the new *Tropical Fruit Recipes.*

Rather than reprint the old book, an extensive revision has been made. Many of the old recipes were retained but new ones have also been added. As a result of members' experiences a number of unusual uses for fruits are also included in this new edition.

PHOTO CREDITS

Contents

Akee

Only fruits picked from the tree immediately after they have turned red and split open should be used. Both immature and overmature fruits are poisonous. The firm and oily white aril surrounding the shiny black seeds is the only edible portion and can be used fresh or cooked. Care should be taken to discard the poisonous pink or purplish membrane near the seed, which is also poisonous. Although the akee is grown on many Caribbean islands and sparsely in South Florida, it is widely used in Jamaica.

AKEE ON TOAST

Remove the white arils from six firm open akee pods. Simmer for five minutes; pour off the water. Add salted water and cook gently until tender. Strain and mash until they look like scrambled eggs. Add any of the following: grated cheese, roasted and chopped cashews, peeled and chopped tomatoes, mashed anchovies, or salt and pepper to taste. Pile the akee mixture on toast and garnish with finely chopped parsley.

AKEE SOUFFLE

1 cup akee arils	½ tsp. salt
3 Tbsp. butter	¼ tsp. white pepper
3 Tbsp. flour	1 cup water
1 cup milk	1 tsp. Worcestershire sauce
4 egg yolks	4 egg whites

Simmer akee arils in water for ten minutes. Drain thoroughly. Melt butter over moderate heat. Stir in flour. Add milk and cook until mixture thickens. Add seasonings. Remove from heat. Beat in egg yolks, one at a time. Stir in akee and let mixture cool to room temperature. Heat oven to 375°. Butter a deep casserole. Beat egg whites until stiff enough to form peaks. Fold the egg whites into the akee mixture. Pour the souffle mixture into the casserole. Bake for about 35 minutes until the top is lightly brown.

CURRIED AKEE

Clean the white arils of 8 to 12 open akee pods, removing all connective tissue. Boil arils until tender but not to the point of breaking. Drain the water off. Blend 1 Tbsp. butter, salt to taste, and 1 Tbsp. curry powder. Add 1/3 cup milk and mix well. Drop akees into the hot sauce, warm, and serve on toast points or as a dip.

Antidesma

The globose or ovoid fruits are ½ inch in diameter, are borne in clusters, and are purplish-red when ripe. Each fruit contains a single seed in juicy pulp. The subacid juice stains fingers and clothes. Antidesma fruit makes excellent juice, jam, and jelly but is seldom eaten out of hand. Jelly making requires the addition of pectin.

ANTIDESMA BUTTER

Pick the clusters of fruit while they are still red. Wash and remove stems. Put in a pan with enough water to cover fruit and cook until the fruit is tender. Mash well and force through a sieve. Measure pulp. Add 1 cup of sugar to each 3 cups of pulp and cook until it thickens, stirring often. To test, remove a small portion of pulp and place in a saucer. When it holds together in a mound, the butter is done. Remove from heat and pour into sterilized jars. Seal at once.

ANTIDESMA JELLY

Prepare fruit as for butter recipe above, except when the cooked fruit is tender, strain through a jelly bag, *not* forcing the pulp through.

Use 4 cups of juice with 7 cups of sugar and bring to a rolling boil. Add 1 bottle liquid pectin and boil 1 minute. Remove from heat, skim, and pour into sterilized jars. Seal at once.

ANTIDESMA JUICE

Prepare fruit as for butter recipe above, and strain through jelly bag as for jelly. This juice may be sweetened and used in various ways. Use 3 cups of juice with 1 cup of sugar and bring to a boil. Pour into sterilized jars and seal. Place on a rack in a large boiler. Add water to cover the tops of jars. Bring to a boil and boil for five minutes. Remove from water, cool, and store in a dark place.

FROZEN ANTIDESMA

Wash the fruit, remove the seeds, and reduce to a pulp in an electric blender. Sweeten to taste, seal in appropriate containers, and then freeze. It can be used later in drinks or as an ice-cream sauce.

Avocado

This attractive fruit has a delicate nut-like flavor. The West Indian varieties generally used in Florida have about half the fat content of the Guatemalan/Mexican varieties raised in California. Half a medium-sized avocado has about the calories of one serving of lean meat.

The fruit does not ripen until it is picked or falls from the tree. A favorite way to use avocados is in salads because they go well with other fruits and vegetables with a wide range of seasonings. In Latin America avocados are often served to each guest to be spooned from the shell into soups or stews to provide a delightful zesty flavor.

AVOCADO ASPIC I

1 Tbsp. gelatin	1 cup boiling water
2 cups avocado pulp	1 Tbsp. lime juice
½ cup cold water	Salt, cayenne

Soak the gelatin in the cold water, add boiling water. Add other ingredients, chill in mold, serve with mayonnaise.

AVOCADO ASPIC II

1 Tbsp. gelatin	1 medium avocado
½ cup cold water	2 tomatoes
1½ cups boiling water	2 Tbsp. sugar
2 Tbsp. lime juice	

Soak the gelatin in the cold water, add boiling water. Add lime juice, sugar, and chill until syrupy. Stir in diced tomato and avocado; pour into mold. Chill.

AVOCADO CAKE

1⅓ cups sugar	1½ tsp. baking soda
½ cup butter	⅓ cup buttermilk
2 eggs	¼ cup golden raisins
1 cup mashed avocado	¼ cup chopped nuts
½ tsp. each: cinnamon, salt,	½ cup chopped dates
allspice, nutmeg	1½ cups flour

Cream sugar, butter, eggs, and avocado until light. Beat in spices, salt, and soda. Add buttermilk, dates, raisins, and nuts. Stir in flour. Bake in 9" x 13" cake pan for 1 hour at 300°.

AVOCADO CREAM

3 oz. cream cheese	1 Tbsp. cointreau (opt.)
¼ cup lime juice	2 cups mashed avocado
½ cup sugar	3 oranges, peeled and sectioned

Mash cream cheese with fork, add lime juice, sugar, and cointreau. Beat until smooth and fluffy. Add avocado to cream cheese mixture and beat until it is light and fluffy. Chill. Arrange 3 or 4 orange sections in a serving glass, heap avocado mixture in the center.

AVOCADO DRESSING

1 clove garlic	¼ tsp. salt
1 small avocado	Pepper
¼ cup lime juice	

Rub bowl with cut garlic clove. Peel avocado, slice, and mash. Whip until it is creamy, adding lime juice gradually. Add seasonings. Serve with tomato or raw mixed vegetable salad.

AVOCADO FRUIT SALAD

1 avocado	½ cup toasted, shredded coconut
½ cup halved seeded grapes	Lettuce
2 cups grapefruit sections	Red or green cherries

Cut avocados in half but do not peel. Scoop out halves with French ball cutter or teaspoon. Combine with grapes and grapefruit. Marinate in French dressing which has been seasoned with chopped mint leaves. Pile into scooped out shells. Arrange on lettuce. Sprinkle with toasted coconut. Garnish with cherries.

AVOCADO ICE CREAM

2 or 3 medium size avocados	1 (13 oz.) can evaporated milk
⅓ cup lime juice	1 can condensed milk
1 cup granulated sugar	½ pt. whipping cream (whipped)
4 whole eggs	1 pt. milk

Whip the avocados and sugar in blender, making sure the sugar is well blended. Then add eggs one at a time and continue to mix while adding remaining ingredients, mixing very well. Freeze.

AVOCADO - PINEAPPLE SHERBET

1 medium avocado	½ cup lemon juice
¾ cup milk	2 egg whites
1 cup sugar	¼ cup sugar
1 cup pineapple juice or crushed pineapple	½ tsp. salt

Puree avocado in blender, add milk, one cup sugar and salt. Stir until sugar is dissolved. Add lemon juice and pineapple. Freeze in trays until mushy. Beat egg whites stiff, slowly adding ¼ cup sugar. Fold into avocado mixture and return to freezer tray.

AVOCADO SALAD

2 medium tomatoes, diced	2 medium avocados
1 Tbsp. onion, minced	Lime juice
2 Tbsp. celery, diced	¼ cup mayonnaise
¼ cup cucumbers, peeled and diced	Lettuce

Combine first four ingredients. Peel and cut avocados into cubes. Sprinkle immediately with lime juice. Add cubed avocados to vegetable mixture. Add mayonnaise and toss to coat. Serve on bed of lettuce.

AVOCADO SOUFFLE

1 medium avocado	½ tsp. salt
2 Tbsp. butter	½ tsp. white pepper
4 Tbsp. flour	3 eggs, separated
½ cup milk	

Peel and mash the avocado. Melt butter, stir in flour, then milk, and make a thick white sauce. Cool mixture, stir in egg yolks, and beat well. Beat egg whites until stiff, fold them into sauce mixture, fold in avocado. Season to taste. Pour into a greased deep dish. Bake in a quick oven (400°) until well risen and golden brown — about 30 min. Serve at once.

AVOCADO WHIP

1 cup avocado puree	2 Tbsp. sugar
1 Tbsp. lime juice	1 pt. vanilla ice cream

Puree avocado in blender and stir in juice, sugar, and ice cream. Mix until smooth. Place in freezing tray and chill but do not freeze.

AVOCADO WITH CREAMED FISH

2 Tbsp. fat or cooking oil	½ to ¾ cup canned salmon or tuna
2 Tbsp. flour	2 medium sized avocados
1 cup milk	½ tsp. salt

Heat fat or oil. Add flour and stir until blended. Then stir in milk slowly until sauce is thickened. Add salt, fish, and seasoning if desired (see below). Cook to heat fish. Cut avocados lengthwise and remove seeds. Fill with creamed fish and heat in 350° oven about 10 minutes.

Additional seasonings: 1. Two or three tsp. curry powder added with the flour to sauce. Serve with cooked rice and mango chutney. 2. Add chopped fresh dill to taste as sauce cooks.

CHILLED AVOCADO SOUP

3 ripe avocados, peeled and coarsely chopped	¼ tsp. onion salt
	Pinch white pepper
1 cup chicken broth	1 tsp. lemon juice
1 cup half-and-half	Lemon slices
1 tsp. salt	

Combine avocado and chicken broth in blender. Blend until smooth. Remove and stir in half-and-half, salt, onion salt, and white pepper. Cover and refrigerate overnight. Before serving, stir in lemon juice and garnish with lemon slices.

CREAM OF AVOCADO SOUP

3 avocados	Salt
2 cups chicken broth	White pepper
1 cup heavy cream	Whipped cream

Peel and puree 2 avocados. Heat in top of double boiler with lightly seasoned chicken broth until boiling. Stir in heavy cream. Keep hot in double boiler. To serve add third avocado, cubed. Season and add a dab of whipped cream to each serving.

DEVILED AVOCADO DIP

Scoop meat from ½ large ripe avocado, leaving shell intact. Mash avocado meat, blend in one family-size can deviled ham, 3 ounces cream cheese, minced parsley, and seasoning to taste. Mix smooth and pile in reserved shell. Serve surrounded with crisp fresh celery, carrot sticks, potato chips, small crackers.

GUACAMOLE

Make a thin paste of one cup mashed avocado, one small finely chopped onion, one clove finely chopped garlic, a dash of Worcestershire sauce, ½ teaspoon olive oil, a dash of paprika, and a little lime juice, salt and pepper to taste. Blend to a smooth consistency.

HOT STUFFED AVOCADO

3 ripe avocados, cut in halves	1 Tbsp. onion, grated
6 Tbsp. lime juice	¼ tsp. celery salt
6 cloves garlic	2 cups cooked chicken pieces
2 Tbsp. butter	Salt and pepper
2 Tbsp. flour	½ cup sharp Cheddar cheese,
1 cup light cream	grated

Place 1 Tbsp. lime juice and a garlic clove in each avocado half. Let stand 30 minutes. Melt butter and blend in flour. Add cream, stirring until thickened. Add onion, celery salt, chicken, and season to taste.

Remove lime juice and garlic from avocado halves, fill with chicken mixture. Sprinkle with grated cheese and place in baking dish containing ½ inch of water. Bake 15 minutes at 350°.

POLYNESIAN AVOCADO DIP

2 or 3 ripe avocados, peeled	Salsa jalapena or green chili peppers
2 or 3 tomatoes, chopped	peeled and chopped
1 medium onion	Wine vinegar or lemon/lime juice

Mash avocados with fork and add remaining ingredients to taste.

SEAFOOD AVOCADO SALAD

1 cup cooked lobster meat	3 avocados, cut in halves
2 cups cooked crabmeat	½ cup mayonnaise
2 cups cooked shrimp	½ cup sour cream
	1 Tbsp. cut chives

Break seafood into bite-size pieces except for a few chunks of lobster and a few shrimp for garnish. Combine seafood and add French dressing to coat. Chill. Just before serving fill avocado halves with seafood mixture. Combine mayonnaise, sour cream, and chives for dressing and spoon over each avocado half. Garnish with shrimp and lobster chunks.

Banana

The banana is one of the few fruits that can be picked full size but green and stored for ripening without loss of flavor. Bunches can be harvested when the fingers have lost their angles and are plump but still green. Hung in a cool shady place they will gradually ripen. The fruit can be used at all stages of ripeness, but the fully ripe, flecked-with-brown stage is best for fruit cups, salads, drinks, desserts, pies, and all baking uses. The "platano," the cooking banana, is a staple of Latin American diet. It is used from the green, very starchy stage to the over-ripe one when the skin is black. (See Plantain, p. 142.)

COOKING BANANAS

Peel slightly green-tipped or all-yellow bananas. Arrange in a greased baking pan. Brush or coat well with melted butter or margerine and lemon juice. Sprinkle lightly with salt. Bake in a very hot oven (450° F.) 10-12 minutes or until bananas are tender. Serve hot as a vegetable or as a dessert.

Peel slightly green-tipped or all-yellow bananas. Arrange on a broiler rack or in a pan. Brush or coat well with melted butter or margerine and lemon juice. Sprinkle lightly with salt. Broil 3 or 4 inches from heat, about 5 minutes each side, or until browned and tender. Serve hot as a vegetable.

Bananas have many uses. Depending on type, they are good raw or cooked, in beverages, with entrees, in quick breads, salads, sandwiches, pies, desserts, cakes, and cookies.

FREEZING BANANAS

Bananas have a marked tendency to darken and lose texture; dipping in lemon juice can prevent darkening. They can then be satisfactorily frozen as a puree.

BANANA BRAN MUFFINS

¼ cup shortening
⅓ to ½ cup sugar
1 egg
1 cup "All Bran" cereal
1½ cups flour
2 tsp. baking powder

½ tsp. salt
½ tsp. soda
½ cup chopped nuts, if desired
1½ cups mashed bananas
2 Tbsp. water
1 tsp. vanilla

Cream shortening and sugar. Add egg and beat well. Add bran and mix thoroughly. Sift flour with baking powder, salt, and soda. Add nuts to flour mixture and add alternately with mashed bananas to which water has been mixed. Stir in vanilla. Pour into oiled muffin plans and bake at 400° for 20 to 25 minutes.

BANANA BREAD

1¾ cups flour, sifted
2¾ tsp. baking powder
½ tsp. salt
⅓ cup shortening

⅔ cup sugar
2 eggs
1 cup ripe banana puree
(See recipe, page 20.)

Sift together flour, baking powder, and salt. Beat shortening in mixing bowl until creamy. Add sugar and eggs. Continue beating at medium speed 1 minute. Add banana puree to egg mixture. Mix until blended. Add flour mixture, beating at low speed for 30 seconds, or only until blended. Do not overbeat. Scrape bowl and beater once or twice. Turn into greased loaf pan and bake in a moderate oven (350°) about 1 hour, or until bread is done. Variations: To egg mixture, add either: 1 cup coarsely chopped nuts, 1 cup seedless raisins, 1 cup finely chopped dates, or ¾ cup of fresh coconut grated or ground.

BANANA CAKE

1¼ cups sugar
½ cup butter
2 eggs
1 tsp. soda

4 Tbsp. sour cream
1 cup banana pulp, mashed
1½ cups pastry flour
1 tsp. vanilla

Cream butter and sugar. Add eggs beaten very light. Add the soda which has been dissolved in the sour cream. Beat well. Add the bananas, pastry flour, and vanilla. Mix well. Pour into a well, buttered oblong pan and bake in a moderate oven, 350° for 30 to 35 mintues. Cool. Frost with favorite lemon, lime, calomondin, or orange frosting.

BANANA CREAM PIE

½ cup sugar
¼ tsp. salt
¼ cup cornstarch or
⅓ cup flour
1 pt. milk

2 eggs, slightly beaten
1 Tbsp. butter or margarine
½ tsp. vanilla
1 baked 9-inch pie shell
3 ripe large bananas

Mix sugar, salt, and cornstarch or flour. Gradually add to milk. Stir over low heat until thick. Stir a small amount of hot mixture into eggs. Then pour back into remaining hot mixture while beating. Continue cooking about 2 minutes, or until thickened. Remove from heat. Add butter or margarine and vanilla. Chill thoroughly. Hot fillings change the flavor of bananas. Line pie shells with a layer of cooled filling. Slice bananas over filling. Cover immediately with remaining filling. Top with whipped cream and banana slices, if desired. Serve immediately.

BANANA ICEBOX CAKE

1 Tbsp. unflavored gelatin
⅓ cup cold water
1¼ cups mashed ripe bananas
¼ to ½ tsp. vanilla
1 tsp. salt

3 Tbsp. lemon juice
½ cup sugar
1¼ cups whipping cream
2 doz. ladyfingers or
sponge cake sliced ½ inch thick

Sprinkle gelatin on cold water and let stand 5 minutes. Then place it over boiling water and add mashed bananas, vanilla, salt, lemon juice, and sugar. Cool until mixture begins to thicken; fold in whipped cream.
   Line bottom and side of pan with ladyfingers or cake slices. Cover with a layer of banana-cream mixture. Alternate layers of cake and banana-cream mixture. Chill thoroughly. Serve with more whipped cream and garnish with jelly.

BANANA OATMEAL COOKIES

¾ cup shortening
1 cup sugar
1 egg
1 cup mashed bananas
1 tsp. salt

1 cup quick-cooking rolled oats
1½ cups flour
½ tsp. soda
¼ tsp. nutmeg
¾ tsp. cinnamon
½ tsp. baking powder

Cream shortening and sugar. Add egg and beat thoroughly. Add banana and rolled oats; mix well. Sift other dry ingredients and stir into mixture. Drop by teaspoonfuls on greased baking sheet about 1½ inches apart. Bake at 400° for 13 to 15 minutes.

BANANA PUREE

Bananas oxidize rapidly when exposed to air so puree should be prepared quickly to avoid the darkening of the fruit. Mash the bananas adding ½ Tbsp. per banana of a sugar syrup prepared as follows: 2 cups of water, ½ cup sugar, ½ tsp. ascorbic acid powder. Mix syrup and mashed bananas well and package in freezer containers. Freeze at once. This puree can be used in any recipe calling for mashed bananas. When thawing, use the puree quickly, even partially frozen.

BANANA SHERBET

2 cups pureed ripe bananas (5 to 6 bananas)	¼ cup white corn syrup
6 Tbsp. lemon juice	$\frac{1}{8}$ tsp. salt
½ cup sugar	1 egg white
	2 cups milk

Mix bananas thoroughly with lemon juice. Add sugar, corn syrup, and salt. Beat egg white until stiff enough to form peaks. Fold into banana mixture. Add milk slowly, stirring constantly. Turn into freezing trays and freeze with indicator at coldest setting. Stir when freezing begins and again just before mixture becomes firm.

BANANAS SINGAPORE

$\frac{1}{3}$ cup margarine or butter	4 bananas, slightly green-tipped
½ cup flour	1½ Tbsp. melted margarine or butter
2 tsp. curry powder	
1 tsp. black pepper	1 to 1½ lbs. shrimp, cooked and cleaned (fresh, frozen, canned)
2¼ cups hot chicken consomme or bouillon	2½ cups cooked rice
½ tsp. salt	

To prepare curry sauce, melt margarine; blend in flour, curry powder, salt, and pepper. Add hot chicken stock, consomme, or bouillon. Cook until thick, stirring constantly. Peel bananas. Keep whole or cut into halves lengthwise or crosswise. Place in greased baking pan. Brush or coat bananas with melted margarine. Pour ½ curry sauce over bananas. Bake in moderate oven (375°) 15 to 18 minutes, or until bananas are tender. Heat shrimp in remaining curry sauce. Serve with bananas on a bed of hot rice.

BANANAS IN RUM CARAMEL

6 Tbsp. sweet butter
¼ cup sugar
4 firm bananas, halved lengthwise

½ cup orange juice
1 Tbsp. grated orange rind
¼ cup dark rum

Cook butter and sugar in a skillet over low heat for five minutes or until sugar begins to carmelize. Add the bananas cut side down and cook them, turning once, until they are almost tender. Add orange juice, orange rind, and shake the pan to deglaze the caramel. Put rum in a small sauce pan. Ignite and pour the flaming sauce over the bananas. Serve with heavy cream or whipped cream.

FIESTA BANANA CAKE

2 cups cake flour, sifted
1 tsp. baking powder
1 tsp. baking soda
¾ tsp. salt
2 eggs, unbeaten
1½ cups sugar

½ cup shortening
½ cup sour milk
  or buttermilk
1 cup mashed ripe bananas
1 tsp. vanilla
½ cup chopped nuts

Measure flour, baking powder, soda, salt, and sugar into sifter. Place shortening in mixing bowl; stir to soften. Sift in dry ingredients. Add ¼ cup milk and mashed bananas. Mix until flour is dampened. Beat 2 minutes in mixer (at low speed). Add the eggs, vanilla, nuts, and remaining milk. Beat 1 minute more. Pour into two round 8 in. layer pans lined with paper. Bake in moderate oven (350°) about 35 to 40 minutes. Cool. Spoon whipped cream between layers and on top of cake. Garnish with banana slices.

HAM BANANA ROLLS WITH CHEESE SAUCE

1½ Tbsp. butter or margarine
2½ Tbsp. flour
¾ cup milk
1½ cups grated sharp Cheddar
  cheese

4 slices cooked, cold ham
Prepared mustard
4 yellow bananas

For cheese sauce, melt butter or margarine; blend in flour. Add milk slowly. Add grated sharp cheese. Stir over low heat until sauce is smooth and thick. Spread each ham slice lightly with mustard. Peel bananas. Wrap one slice of ham around each banana. Place in baking pan. Pour cheese sauce over bananas. Bake in moderate oven (350°) for 30 minutes. Serve hot with cheese sauce from pan.

Barbados Cherry

This fruit is one of the highest sources of ascorbic acid. The bright red, juicy, cherry-like fruits are obscurely 3-lobed; each contains 3 triangular ridged seeds. Two or three crops are produced yearly. Fruits are quite acid and make excellent punches, preserves, and jellies. Juice freezes well, retaining its color, flavor, and vitamin content. To juice, a food mill is the best tool; for clear juice put the puree through a jelly bag. Ice cubes prepared with puree provide a ready punch base if kept in freezer containers.

BARBADOS CHERRY BUTTER

Prepare the cherries as for jelly (see recipe below), except instead of allowing the juice to drip through a jelly bag, rub the cooked fruit through a strainer to remove the seeds. Measure the puree and add ¾ cup of sugar for each cup of pulp. Cook rapidly until a small amount cooled will hold its shape. Pour into sterilized jars and seal.

BARBADOS CHERRY JELLY

4 cups cherry juice	2 Tbsp. lemon or lime juice
5 cups sugar	1 pkg. powdered pectin

Wash and measure cherries. Add equal parts of water and fruit to a heavy sauce pan. When boiling starts, stir, mash, and cook about 20 minutes. Pour into cloth jelly bag and allow to drip for several hours.

To cook into jelly, use a large kettle and combine 4 cups of juice with 1 package of powdered pectin and 2 tablespoons of lemon or lime juice. Boil one minute. Add sugar. Bring to rolling boil for one minute. Pour into jars and seal.

BARBADOS CHERRY JUICE

Pick some underripe fruit along with the bright red ones. Wash and stem the cherries. Cut open to make sure they are sound. Place in a saucepan with enough water to barely cover the fruit. Cook slowly, mashing the fruit as it gets tender. Pour this into a jelly bag and allow juice to drip through. Do not add sugar. Freeze until used.

BARBADOS CHERRY MASH

Wash berries, take off stems. If stems are left on, flavor is impaired. Place berries in sauce pan and boil for 30 minutes. Pass through a food mill or heavy strainer. For each quart of mash add 2 cups of sugar and ½ cup of white Karo syrup. Heat gently and stir to dissolve sugar. Freeze in appropriate container.

BARBADOS CHERRY MASH FLIP

To a tall glass add the following:

1 jigger white rum   3 jiggers soda water
2 jiggers Barbados Cherry Mash
  (see recipe above)

Stir well and add ice.

BARBADOS CHERRY PRESERVES

1 pound Barbados cherries   3 cups sugar
Water

Wash cherries thoroughly. Seed cherries. Add water to almost cover. Add sugar. Cook until tender and syrup is thickened. Pour into hot sterilized jars. Seal.

BARBADOS CHERRY PUREE

Select ripe fruit. Mash through a food mill, a few at a time to prevent a large build-up of pits, which inhibits food mill action. The resulting puree can either be sweetened to taste before freezing or not as desired. Frozen in ice trays and bagged for freezer storage the puree can be kept up to a year and forms an excellent base for fruit punches.

TROPICAL PUNCH

Barbados cherry juice and pulp   Pineapple juice
Rangpur lime juice   Gingerale

Use equal proportions of the above ingredients. Serve chilled. Some sugar may be added if mixture is too tart. Rum may be added if desired. Serve over crushed ice.

Black Sapote

The olive-green fruits vary in size from a softball to half again larger. The fruit does not change color when mature. It should be watched carefully as it can be hard one day, soft and ready the next. To remove the brownish-black pulp, cut from blossom and toward stem into 4-6 wedges. With spoon gently scoop out pulp, discarding seeds and undeveloped arils. The ripe rind tends to break up easily. Pulp can be used immediately or frozen. It keeps well frozen. Some people find the taste to be like chocolate. Flavor is enhanced by the addition of a little vanilla or rum.

BLACK SAPOTE BREAD

1 cup sugar	2 cups quick baking mix
¼ cup shortening	¾ cup grated or
2 eggs	ground coconut
1 cup mashed ripe sapote	¼ tsp. vanilla

Cream sugar and shortening. Add beaten eggs, vanilla, and sapote pulp. Mix well. Add baking mix and coconut. Stir until well mixed. Pour into well greased loaf pan. A piece of waxed paper, cut to fit the bottom of the pan, will keep the warm loaf from breaking into pieces when loaf is removed from pan. Bake 50 minutes in oven preheated to 350°. Black sapote bread has a better flavor a day or two after baking. The bread will keep in the refrigerator for two to three weeks.

BLACK SAPOTE CAKE

1 cup milk	1 cup grated coconut
1 large black sapote	1 Tbsp. light cream
1 box yellow cake mix	1 tsp. vanilla
¼ cup chopped nuts	

Heat the milk until hot but not boiling. Remove from heat and add pulp of black sapote. Mix well. Add 1 tsp. vanilla and the cake mix. Beat until well blended. Pour into a greased and floured 9 by 13 inch pan. Sprinkle the top of cake with chopped nuts. Bake 45 minutes at 350°.

Remove cake from oven. Cover the top of cake with 1 cup coconut mixed with the cream. Spread on top of cake and put cake under the broiler until coconut is toasted. Cool in pan. This makes a moist cake.

BLACK SAPOTE ICE BOX CAKE

Put a rounded Tbsp. of Black Sapote Mousse (see recipe below) on each round sugar cookie. Stack cookies on edge in an aluminum loaf pan. Press out air pockets. Cover top of cookies with wax paper. Refrigerate overnight. Ice the cookie log with whipped cream or commercial whip and chill 2 hours. Cut slices diagonally across the log. This will give a striped effect of alternating mousse and cake.

BLACK SAPOTE MOUSSE I

1 cup black sapote pulp	1 tsp. almond flavoring
3 Tbsp. powdered sugar	2 cups whipped cream or
2 Tbsp. brandy or	whipped topping
Creme de Cocoa	

Mix sapote pulp, sugar, brandy, and flavoring together. Fold in the whipped cream. Serve at once or chill in refrigerator tray. Do not freeze!

BLACK SAPOTE MOUSSE II

1 cup black sapote pulp	2 Tbsp. cold water
¾ cup sugar	3 Tbsp. boiling water
Sprinkle of salt	1 pt. cream, beaten stiff
1 tsp. gelatin	1 or 2 Tbsp. Grand Marnier

Soak gelatin in cold water. Mash pulp until it is smooth. Add sugar and mix well. Add gelatin which has been dissolved in the hot water. Chill until thickened. Beat until light. Fold in the whipped cream using a wire whisk. Pour into a refrigerator tray and freeze.

HONEY BLACK SAPOTE CAKE

3 large sapotes	2 tsp. baking powder
½ cup margerine	1 tsp. vanilla
1 cup honey	2 tsp. cinnamon
3 eggs	½ tsp. pwd. cloves
1½ cups sifted whole wheat flour	½ tsp. baking soda
¼ tsp. salt	1/3 cup pwd. milk

Cream margerine and honey and gradually add egg yolks and sapotes. Sift and then add dry ingredients a little at a time. Then fold in beaten egg whites. Pour into greased 8 x 12 inch baking plan. Bake for 45 minutes at 350°F. Test cake with toothpick inasmuch as baking time may vary somewhat according to the size (quantity) of sapotes. Serve with a dollop of Cool Whip for a different, delicious cake.

Breadfruit

Breadfruit is a dietary staple in many tropical areas. Captain Bligh of the *Bounty* transported breadfruit seedlings from the South Pacific to the West Indies. Mature fruit is roundish or ovoid and may weigh 2 to 10 pounds. The yellowish green rind is divided into many low, sometimes spiny, projections. The edible portion is the white to yellowish pulp of slightly immature fruit. The large central core is discarded. Fully ripe fruit is soft and yellow to brownish. Boiled or raw the fruit can be frozen in suitable containers.

BAKED BREADFRUIT

1 very ripe breadfruit   ½ cup butter
1 cup water

Place whole breadfruit in a shallow pan, add water and bake at 300° F. for 3 hours. Peel and cut into 6 sections, removing stem and core. Top with butter and serve sprinkled with lemon juice and cinnamon.

BREADFRUIT AND COCONUT PUDDING

3 cups ripe breadfruit   1 coconut, grated
½ cup sugar   1 cup boiling water
½ tsp. salt

Pour boiling water over coconut, allow to stand 15 minutes and squeeze through cloth. Remove core from a soft ripe breadfruit and scrape out pulp. Add coconut milk and sugar. Pour into buttered baking dish and bake at 350° for about 1 hour. Canned grated coconut could be used instead of fresh coconut. Canned coconut is usually sweetened, in which case the amount of sugar needed will be less than ½ cup.

BREADFRUIT BREAD

1 cup very ripe breadfruit   ½ tsp. salt
1¾ cups flour   ½ cup sugar
2 tsp. baking powder   1 egg
¼ tsp. soda   ⅓ cup cooking oil
¼ tsp. nutmeg   1 cup milk

Put egg, oil, and milk in mixing bowl and mix well. Add the breadfruit and mix thoroughly. Measure and sift all dry ingredients. Sift dry ingredients into the liquid ingredients. Mix until smooth. Pour into buttered loaf pan. Bake at 325° for one hour.

28

BREADFRUIT COO-COO

1 breadfruit
¼ to ½ lb. cooked and
  seasoned ground meat

2 tsp. salt
½ cup water or stock

Boil, peel, and mash the breadfruit. Mix all ingredients together and heat. Stir continuously until all liquid has boiled away. Serve in a buttered dish.

BREADFRUIT FRITTERS

½ cup ripe breadfruit
2⅔ cups flour
6 tsp. baking powder

1 teaspoon salt
1⅓ cups milk
3 eggs

Remove core of breadfruit and scoop out pulp. Mash fruit and add dry ingredients. Beat eggs until light, add milk, and mix. Combine liquid and dry mixtures. Drop batter by spoonfuls into hot fat and fry until golden brown. Drain on paper towels. Serve with honey or any fruit syrup.

BREADFRUIT PIE

2 cups breadfruit, cooked
  and pureed
½ cup sugar
½ tsp. salt
½ tsp. nutmeg

½ tsp. ground ginger
3 eggs, separated
1 cup milk
½ cup cream

Mix all ingredients except egg whites. Beat egg whites until stiff, then fold into mixture. Pour into a greased dish and bake at 350° for 45 minutes. Or, pour into unbaked pie shell, bake at 400° for 15 minutes, then lower heat to 350° for another 30 minutes.

BREADFRUIT PUDDING SAVORY

4 cups crushed breadfruit
½ cup milk
1 egg, beaten

1 onion, minced
Pepper and salt
2 oz. butter

Mix seasoning with breadfruit. Add beaten egg and warm milk. Stir in butter. Place in greased baking dish and brown in moderate (350°) oven.

BREADFRUIT SALAD

1 large green bread'fruit cooked   ½ cup nuts
1 cup celery   1 tsp. mustard
½ cup onion   Salt and pepper
3 hard cooked eggs   Mayonnaise

Cut breadfruit into ¾ inch chunks. Marinate in French dressing. Chop celery, onions, eggs and nuts. Mix all ingredients lightly and add enough mayonnaise to moisten. Add seasonings to taste. Chill before serving. A small can of tuna may be added to this salad if desired.

BREADFRUIT TUNA PATTIES

½ mature green breadfruit,   1 medium onion, chopped
  beginning to soften   Salt and pepper
1 can (6½ oz.) chunk tuna, drained   Corn flake crumbs or buttered
1 egg, beaten   crumbs

Cook breadfruit and mash. Mash drained tuna and add with onion to breadfruit. Add beaten egg and stir all together. Salt and pepper to taste. Form into patties and cover with corn-flake crumbs. Fry in small amount of cooking oil until both sides are light brown.

Serve hot with chopped parsley, green onions, or wedges of lemon. If sauce is desired, warm mayonnaise thinned with a little lemon juice.

FRIED BREADFRUIT

Peel ripe breadfruit, cut into slices and remove core. Sprinkle with salt, pepper, chives and allow to stand 5 to 10 minutes. Fry in hot oil, sprinkle with bread crumbs, and serve hot.

GOLDEN BREADFRUIT

1 ripe breadfruit, peeled and diced   2 Tbsp. butter
½ cup water   ½ tsp. salt
2 cups diced carrots, cooked   Pepper to taste

Cook breadfruit in water until tender. Do not drain. Combine with carrots and mash together with butter and seasonings. Serve hot.

SCALLOPED BREADFRUIT WITH CHEESE SAUCE

1 mature green breadfruit

Peel and slice breadfruit. Let stand in cold water for one half hour. Put breadfruit slices in layers in a buttered casserole. Dot each layer with butter and sprinkle with salt and pepper to taste. Cover with cheese sauce and bake ½ hour at 350°.

CHEESE SAUCE

1 Tbsp. chopped onion	1½ cups milk
1 Tbsp. butter	1 cup grated cheddar cheese
1 Tbsp. flour	¼ tsp. dry mustard

Heat butter in heavy sauce pan. Add chopped onion and sautee until yellow. Stir in flour. Add milk. Heat to boiling and add cheese. Remove from heat and stir until cheese melts. Pour sauce over the breadfruit.

STEAMED BREADFRUIT

Remove stem, core, and also the rind, if desired, from a soft-ripe breadfruit. Cut into halves or quarters, place on pan, and steam in covered steamer until thoroughly cooked (1 to 2 hours). Season with margerine, salt, and pepper.

Note: Breadfruit may be steamed in a pressure cooker for 10 to 15 minutes at 15 pounds pressure for very soft fruit. Firm fruit should be cooked 20 to 30 minutes depending upon the degree of ripeness.

STUFFED BREADFRUIT

1 breadfruit, full size but not ripe	1 tomato
	1 small onion
½ lb. ground beef or pork	2-3 blades chives
1 Tbsp. butter or oil	
Salt and pepper	

Peel and parboil breadfruit whole in salted water. Lightly fry meat and seasonings in the butter. Cool breadfruit and remove core and a little fruit from the stalk end. Fill the hole with the meat mixture. Bake in a moderate oven until soft and brown (about 45 minutes). Butter crust and serve hot.

Butia Palm

The *Butia capitata* is graceful, with arching gray-green foliage. It is a quite hardy tree that can survive north to the Florida-Georgia line. Its large clusters of fruit are green until late summer or early fall when they color up and soften.

Fruits are globose to ovoid, yellowish or reddish, about 1 inch in diameter with pulpy-fibrous or rather soft exterior. The flesh may be peeled off and eaten, prepared as a soft puree, or used for jelly. Left on the tree the fruit ripens a few at a time. If the entire cluster is cut off at the time that it starts to ripen and stored in a cool place, all the fruits will ripen at one time after a few days.

BUTIA PALM FRUIT FLUFF PIE

1 graham cracker pie shell
¾ cup Butia Palm fruit puree
  (see recipe below)
2 Tbsp. unflavored gelatin
¼ cup cold water

1¼ cups boiling water
½ cup sugar
⅛ tsp. salt
⅔ cup chilled undiluted evap.
  milk, whipped
6 small slices canned pineapple

Chill a prepared graham cracker pie crust. Then make the filling by combining the palm fruit puree, gelatin, and cold water. Add boiling water and sugar and stir until gelatin is dissolved. Chill until partially set. Whip with electric mixer on medium speed until mixture is fluffy. Fold in whipped evaporated milk. Pour into crust and chill until firm. Garnish with rings of sliced pineapple.

BUTIA PALM FRUIT JELLY

2 cups prepared palm
Fruit juice

3¼ cups sugar
½ cup liquid fruit pectin

Barely cover palm fruit with water and boil for about 5 minutes. Crush fruit and strain through a jelly bag. Add sugar to juice and bring to a boil over high heat, stirring constantly. At once stir in pectin. Bring to a full rolling boil for 1 minute, stirring constantly. Remove from heat, skim off foam, and pour quickly into hot clean jars and seal.

BUTIA PALM FRUIT PUREE

Wash palm fruit and remove seeds. Fill blender about half full with fruit pieces. Chop until very fine puree. Strain fruit if fibers are present.

Use Butia Palm fruit puree sweetened as topping for ice cream, sweetened and mixed with mayonnaise for fruit salad dressing, or for base of other recipes. The puree may be frozen for later use.

BUTIA SALAD

1 Tbsp. unflavored gelatin	1 cup boiling water
¾ cup Butia Palm fruit puree	3 medium bananas, sliced
(see recipe p. 33)	1 cup creamed cottage cheese
½ cup sugar	¼ cup pecans

Combine gelatin, ½ palm fruit puree, and sugar. Mix well and allow to stand while heating water. Add 1 cup boiling water and stir until gelatin is dissolved.

Add remaining puree and sliced bananas. Chill until firm in ring mold. Serve on a bed of leaf lettuce or curly endive. Combine chopped pecans with cottage cheese and pile in center. Reserve several pecan halves for garnishing.

MANGO AND BUTIA UPSIDE-DOWN CAKE

2 cups fresh mango slices	1 small pkg. white cake mix
1 cup Butia Palm fruit puree	or ½ large pkg.
(see recipe p. 33)	1 egg
1 cup sugar	Water (as directed on cake mix
2 Tbsp. quick cooking tapioca	package)

Combine mango slices, palm fruit puree, sugar, and tapioca. Generously butter a 10 x 14 inch pan. Spread mango-palm fruit mixture over the bottom. Mix white cake according to directions on package and spread evenly in baking pan. Bake at 350° about 40 minutes. Serve hot with whipped cream or topping, if desired.

UNCOOKED BUTIA PALM FRUIT JAM

2 cups Butia Palm fruit puree	½ cup liquid pectin
(see recipe p. 33)	3 cups sugar

Mix 3 cups of sugar and palm fruit puree and allow to stand about half an hour. Stir in liquid pectin and continue stirring about 3 minutes. Pour into freezer containers at once, leaving ½ inch headspace. Allow to stand covered for 24 hours. Store in refrigerator if jam is to be used within about three weeks. If to be kept longer, seal and store in freezer.

Note: Uncooked jam has a nice consistency. It spreads easily. If weeping occurs, stirring will blend it. Do not keep in the refrigerator longer than 4 weeks or in the freezer longer than 3 months.

Calamondin

This close relative of citrus produces small, dark yellowish-orange fruits resembling small tangerines. They are seedy and highly acid so their major use is in marmalades.

CALAMONDIN CAKE

1 pkg. lemon or orange cake mix	1 cup calamondin puree
1 pkg. lemon gelatin	4 eggs
1/3 cup milk	½ cup cooking oil
	2 tsp. lemon extract

Wash and seed fruit. Place in blender and puree, leaving some small pieces. Combine cake mix and gelatin, mixing well. Combine extract, puree, and oil. Add to batter and mix well. Bake in greased pan at 350° until cake begins to leave sides of pan. Glaze while still hot.

Glaze

6 Tbsp. soft butter	2 tsp. lemon extract
3 cups confectioners sugar	1 cup calamondin puree

Combine butter and sugar; mix well. Add lemon extract and puree. Add more sugar if necessary to make medium consistency.

CALAMONDIN-KUMQUAT MARMALADE

1 cup prepared sliced calamondin fruit (see recipe, p. 39)	8 cups water
	4 cups sugar (or, 1 cup sugar to 1 cup mixed fruit)
3 cups sliced kumquats	

Prepare kumquats by washing, slicing thinly and removing seeds. Combine fruit and water. Cook 20 minutes, or until kumquats are tender. Allow to stand overnight.

Cook mixed fruit for 10 minutes and add sugar in equal portions. Cook quickly to 220°, or until boiling liquid sheets on spoon. Store in sterilized jars if kept more than a week.

CALAMONDIN MARMALADE I

4 cups prepared calamondin (see recipe, p. 39)	3 cups sugar

Remove seeds from prepared fruit and grind pulp medium coarse, or put through food chopper, or cut into very thin slices.

Measure 4 cups of fruit and bring to boil. Add 3 cups of sugar, stirring to dissolve. Cook until syrup sheets on spoon, about 220°. Remove from heat and let stand until 175°, or bubbling stops. Pour into sterilized jars and seal at once.

CALAMONDIN MARMALADE II

4 lb. calamondin	6 oz. liquid pectin
2½ lb. sugar	

Wash fruit in warm soapy water and rinse well. Cut in half and remove seeds. Chop or puree fruit in a blender. Cook fruit over medium high heat until mixture thickens. Add sugar and cook 15 minutes longer. Add pectin, remove from heat, and put in jars and seal.

FLORIDA FRUIT MARMALADE

4 medium oranges	Water
12 calamondins	1 can (No. 2) crushed pineapple
12 kumquats	1 jar (6 oz.) maraschino cherries,
1 lemon	chopped
1 grapefruit	Sugar

Wash and dry each piece of fruit; remove blemishes and seeds. Cut in pieces small enough to force into grinder. To each cup of ground fruits, add two and one-half cups water. Let stand overnight in cool place. Cook until fruits are soft; add pineapple and cherries. Add one-half cup sugar to each cup fruit used. Cook until syrup sheets from a spoon. Pack in sterile jars; seal.

PICKLED CALAMONDINS

3 cups sugar	Cloves
1 cup vinegar (or less)	Prepared calamondins
½ oz. stick cinnamon	(see recipe, p. 39)

Make a syrup of sugar, vinegar, cinnamon, and cloves. Pour the hot syrup over the preserved fruit and let stand until the following day. Heat to boiling. Put in jars and seal.

PREPARED CALAMONDIN

2 Tbsp. baking soda for each quart of fruit	Boiling water Cold water

Choose well-colored fruit, but not overripe. Clip off stems. Wash thoroughly and rub off skin blemishes with soft cloth. Place fruit in container and sprinkle with baking soda. Cover with boiling water and let stand 10 minutes. Pour off soda water and rinse well in 3 or 3 changes of cold water. Puncture each fruit through lengthwise with long needle, making 5 or 6 punctures.

QUICK CALAMONDIN MARMALADE

8 cups calamondins, halved and seeded	5 cups water 16 cups sugar

Place 3 cups of water into blender and fill with calamondin halves. Chop at low speed, or flick on and off until calamondin peel is shredded. Pour into large cooking pot. Continue until all fruit is chopped.

Bring rapidly to a boil, remove from heat, and add all the sugar. Return to heat and bring to boil again. Boil rapidly until first signs of jelling are noticed — not to point of sheeting on spoon because it will become too solid later. Pour into sterilized jars and seal.

WHOLE PRESERVED CALAMONDINS

1 qt. prepared calamondins (see recipe, above) Water as needed	2 lbs. sugar 1 qt. water

Place prepared fruit into pan and cover with cold water. Boil gently until toothpick will puncture skin easily.

Prepare thin syrup by boiling ingredients (right column above) in saucepan with tight cover. Lift calamondins from boiling water and drop into boiling syrup. Boil gently with pan partly covered until fruit looks translucent. Place cover on pan, remove from heat, and allow to stand covered tightly for 24 hours.

Reheat to boiling. Pack in sterilized jars. Cover with strained syrup. Seal jars and place in hot water to cover completely. Heat to boiling for 10 minutes.

Canistel

This fruit is pointed, orange-yellow, globose or ovoid, 2 to 5 inches long, and smooth skinned. The orange-colored, sweetish, mealy pulp contains 1 to 3 dark-brown shiny seeds. There is considerable variation in size, shape, and flavor of the fruit.

CANISTEL AND SWEET POTATO PUDDING

1½ cups grated or finelh
  chopped raw sweet potatoes
½ cup mashed canistel
⅓ cup brown sugar
¼ cup honey
2 eggs

½ tsp. salt
½ tsp. nutmeg
¼ tsp. cloves
2 cups milk
⅓ cup butter

Peel raw sweet potatoes and grate them finely or put them through the food chopper twice, using the fine blade. Combine eggs, sugar, honey, salt, and spices. Heat milk and stir in grated sweet potatoes and butter. Cook just long enough to heat potatoes; add canistel. Combine the egg mixture and the canistel mixture. Mix well. Pour into an 8 x 8 x 2 inch baking pan. Bake 2 hours in a slow oven (300°). Serve warm.

CANISTEL CREAM

1 Tbsp. gelatin
¼ cup cold water
½ cup boiling water
½ cup orange juice

½ cup finely mashed canistel
½ cup sugar
1 cup heavy cream

Soak gelatin in cold water and dissolve in boiling water. Add sugar and mix well. Cool. Add orange juice and canistel. Chill until syrupy. Whip cream and fold into canistel mixture. Pour into mold and chill. Serve as dessert.

CANISTEL CUSTARD

¾ cup ripe fruit mashed
½ cup sugar
3 eggs

¼ tsp. salt
2¼ cups milk (scalded)
1 Tbsp. lime juice

Beat eggs lightly. Stir in sugar, fruit, and lime juice. Add hot milk slowly while stirring. Pour into buttered custard cups. Set in pan of hot water about 1 inch deep. Bake at 350° (about 30-40 minutes) until custard is done.

CANISTEL FLAVORED ICE CREAM

½ cup canistel pulp   2 cups vanilla ice cream

Peel ripe fruit and mash or grate to make pulp. Soften ice cream slightly and add pulp, mixing thoroughly. Place into container and freeze.

CANISTEL FRUIT CUP

Combine with one or two fresh fruits of contrasting texture and flavor. Add light sugar syrup and serve chilled as first course or dessert.

CANISTEL MILKSHAKE

Peel ripe fruit and mix in the blender with some milk or cream until it is like a smooth custard. It is delicious this way. A little rum is a good addition, or use ½ cup of canistel cream (see recipe, p. 39), 1 cup milk, and about ½ cup vanilla ice cream. Mix in blender. Add 1 to 2 teaspoons orange liqueur. Serve at once.

CANISTEL PIE

Mix together: Mix together:
⅞ cup brown sugar   1½ cups mashed canistel pulp
1 tsp. ground cinnamon   2 well beaten eggs
1 tsp. ground ginger   2 Tbsp. orange juice
½ tsp. salt   1¼ cups milk

Blend two mixtures together. Pour into prepared, unbaked pie shell. Bake at 450° for 10 minutes. Reduce heat to 250° and bake 50 minutes longer. Serve warm or chilled, with whipped cream.

CANISTEL SAUCE

8 large canistel   Sugar
¾ cup milk or sweet cream

Put fruit through colander or into blender after peeling. Combine with milk. Add sugar to taste. May be used as a pudding, or as a dessert topping for ice cream or rice pudding.

Carambola

This fruit, 4 to 6 inches long, is ovoid to ellipsoid and has 4-6 strong longitudenal ribs. When cut across, the resulting star shape leads to the popular name of star fruit. The flesh is crisp, juicy, and aromatic, is covered by a thick waxy cuticle, and in most varieties is quite acid. Varieties being propagated by the Rare Fruit Council, however, are less acid and much more desirable for use in drinks, jellies, jams, and in fresh fruit salads.

CARAMBOLA BUTTER

Slice carambolas and remove seeds. Mash enough of the fruit to extract some of the juice. Cook until soft, about 20 minutes. Mash the pulp, and pour into a saucepan. For each cup of carambola pulp add 2/3 cup sugar. Cook, stirring to prevent scorching, until slightly thickened. For a thick butter add 1 Tbsp. liquid pectin just before removing the butter from the heat. Mix well. Pour into jars and seal.

CARAMBOLA DAQUIRI

1 banana	3 Tbsp. honey
1 lime	6 oz. rum
6 carambolas (seeded)	

Blend above ingredients. Chill.

CARAMBOLA FRUIT CUP

Carambola may be combined with other fruits (canned as well as fresh) to make an attractive and delicious appetizer.

CARAMBOLA GARNISH

Saute carambola slices lightly in butter. Sprinkle with brown sugar and use as a garnish for beef or pork roast.

Put slices of carambola on fish which is to be baked or broiled.

CARAMBOLA JELLY

Break up and heat fresh fruit 30 to 40 minutes. Use no water. Press.

Bring to full rolling boil:
3 cups juice
3 cups sugar
1½ Tbsp. lime juice
Add:
½ bottle liquid pectin
Do not double the recipe

Return to full boil, stirring constantly for one minute. Skim and pour into hot sterilized jars. Seal at once.

CARAMBOLA JUICE

2 quarts sliced carambola

Wash carambola carefully in cold water. Cut into small pieces. Blender chop a few pieces at a time until carambolas are converted into a thick puree. Strain juice through a fine sieve. Serve carambola juice as carambolade (see recipe, p. 47), or as punch (see recipe, p. 46).

CARAMBOLA PICKLES

4 cups carambola slices
1½ cups sugar
½ cup vinegar

1 stick cinnamon
½ tsp. whole cloves

Place carambola slices in glass jar or bowl. Make a syrup of sugar, vinegar, and spices. Bring to boil, pour over carambola slices. Let stand overnight. Next day, drain off syrup, bring again to boil. Place carambola slices in hot, sterilized jars and pour boiling syrup over (to overflowing). Seal. Store in cool place.

CARAMBOLA PIE I

1 cup carambola juice
1 pkg. gelatin (1 Tbsp.)

¼ cup sugar
9 oz. topping mix

Soften gelatin in ¼ cup juice. Dissolve over low heat or hot water. Add remaining carambola juice. Add sugar and mix well. Chill until almost set. Remove from refrigerator and beat until fluffy. Fold into the topping mix. Pour into baked pie shell. Chill. Cut slices of carambola and decorate top for serving.

CARAMBOLA PIE II

1 qt. sliced ripe carambolas	2 Tbsp. butter or margarine
1 cup sugar	Nutmeg to taste
¼ cup quick cooking tapioca	Pastry for 2 pie crusts

Prepare carambolas by cutting off the edges of the ridges. Remove seeds and slice in ½ inch slices. Combine tapioca and sugar and lightly mix with sliced fruit. Line a 9 inch pie pan with pastry. Spread prepared fruit over pastry. Dot with small pieces of butter and sprinkle with nutmeg. Roll the top pastry so it will be large enough to make a good seal. Cut gashes to allow the escape of steam. Bake in pre-heated oven at 425° about 35 minutes or until pastry is golden brown.

CARAMBOLA PUNCH

Sweeten juice (see recipe, p. 45) to taste and freeze in ice cube trays. Serve 2 or 3 frozen carambola cubes in gingerale. Garnish with fresh carambola slices.

CARAMBOLA RELISH

2 cups sliced ripe carambola	1 Tbsp. cider vinegar
¾ cup candied orange peel	¼ cup sugar
¾ cup dried figs	2 Tbsp. candied ginger
1 Tbsp. lemon juice	

Slice carambola and remove seeds. Cut figs and ginger in pieces. Combine all ingredients in electric blender and blend until chopped. Refrigerate overnight before using to allow flavor to develop.

CARAMBOLA SALAD

½ cup chopped nuts	Sugar to taste
½ cup chopped coconut	1 tsp. vanilla
1 cup boiling water	2 3-oz. pkgs. lime Jello
1 cup carambola juice	1 10-oz. bottle 7-Up, gingerale,
1 8-oz. pkg. cream cheese	or Sprite
	2 cups chopped carambola

Dissolve Jello in hot water. Soften cream cheese and add liquids gradually. Stir in nuts, coconut, and chopped carambola. Chill in mold and serve when ready.

CARAMBOLADE

Dilute with water using about 1 cup of juice with 2 cups of water. Add sugar if carambolas are sour. Serve over cracked ice. Garnish with thin carambola slices.

CHICKEN RICE SALAD WITH CARAMBOLA

4 cups cooked rice
1 cup orange segments
1 cup mayonnaise
2 Tbsp. chopped red or green peppers
1 Tbsp. chopped chives
1 cup sliced celery

½ cup sour cream
Salt and pepper
3 cups cooked diced chicken
1 to 2 carambolas
2 Tbsp. toasted almonds, chopped

Cut ribs off carambola and slice. Do not use the center part. Combine mayonnaise and sour cream with salt and pepper to taste. Toss all dry ingredients together except almonds. Pour mayonnaise/sour cream mixture over salad and toss to blend. Garnish with almonds.

GOLD STAR TARTS

First, prepare 15 tart shells (see recipe, p. 172).

Next, prepare fruit for tart shells.

8 oz. cream cheese
⅓ cup sugar
2 tsp. flour
1 egg

1 Tbsp. milk or cream
1 tsp. vanilla
15 slices of carambola about ½ inch thick, seeds removed

Soften cream cheese, stir in sugar and flour. Beat until it is fluffy. Add egg, vanilla, and cream, beating well. (Or simply blend all these ingredients in a blender.) Divide this filling among the 15 cups. Gently press a carambola slice into the filling until the top of the filling and the top of the slice are level. Place pans into a preheated 425° oven. Bake at this temperature for 6 minutes, then lower heat to 250° and bake for 8 minutes more. The appearance of these tarts is best right after baking. May be served warm or cold.

HONEY-CARAMBOLA PRESERVES

Slice ripe carambolas crosswise. Cover with honey and let stand overnight. Next day, cook for 5 minutes, fill sterilized jars, and seal. This makes a delicious preserve with a plum-like flavor.

Carissa

The reddish fruits are ovoid to ellipsoid and up to 2" long. A papery skin covers a reddish pulp with a white milky latex enclosing several almost circular seeds. Flavor is faintly suggestive of raspberry. Sauce made from fully ripe fruit tastes much like that made from cranberry. Cooked juice and pulp have a milky-red appearance but are attractively bright red with sugar. Pans in which carissa is cooked have a sticky latex ring that will not clean off using the usual abrasives. Dissolve the ring by using salad oil or mineral spirits. A latex gum-up will develop in the food waste disposer if carissa residue gets into it. Put salad oil on fingers before working with carissa to avoid stickiness.

CANNED CARISSAS

Select large firm fruit. Wash, peel, and prick, and drop into syrup made of 1 part sugar to 1 part water.

Cook very gently at just below the boiling point for 10 minutes.

Pack into sterilized jars and process for 12 minutes in boiling water bath for pints and 15 minutes for quarts. Use for salads and pies.

CARISSA CREAM

1 Tbsp. gelatin	½ cup sugar
½ cup cold water	Pinch of salt
1 cup boiling carissa juice	1 cup heavy cream, whipped

Soak gelatin in cold water 5 minutes, then dissolve in boiling carissa juice. Add sugar and salt and stir until sugar dissolves. Chill until slightly thickened. Fold in the whipped cream and chill until firm.

CARISSA HORS D'OEUVRE

Wash and drain choice fruit, fresh and ripe; split, remove seeds and put on ice until shortly before serving. Stuff cavities with cottage or cream cheese. Place on a bed of shredded lettuce.

CARISSA ICE CREAM

1 cup carissa pulp
1 cup sugar

2 cups whipping cream

Crush and strain the ripe fruit into a pulp and add sugar. Let stand a few minutes. Whip the cream until it is very stiff, fold into the pulp, and freeze in refrigerator tray. Stir occasionally while freezing.

CARISSA JELLY

4 cups crushed or sliced
  ripe carissa
2 cups water

Sugar (1 cup to each cup of
  strained juice or pulp)

Wash and drain fruit; slice, or crush if fruits are very soft. Add water, bring to boiling point, and simmer until fruit is tender. Drain through jelly bag for a clear jelly, or put through sieve for a jelly with pulp.

Measure juice or juicy pulp; use an equal amount of sugar. Bring juice to boiling point. Add sugar and boil until the mixture sheets from the spoon. Pour into sterilized jelly glasses and seal with paraffin.

CARISSA PIE

1 pt. carissas (sliced crosswise)
1 Tbsp. flour
½ cup sugar

1 Tbsp. butter
½ cup water
Pastry

Slice well-ripened carissa into a deep, buttered baking dish. Mix flour with sugar and sprinkle over the fruit. Dot lightly with butter. Pour water over the mixture. Top with pastry, slit to allow steam to escape, and bake in moderate oven until fruit is cooked and pastry is brown. Serve hot with hard sauce flavored with lemon juice or vanilla.

CARISSA PRESERVES

1 qt. carissas
3 cups sugar

2 cups water

Carissas may be peeled or not. Halve, quarter, or slice crosswise and remove seeds. Make a syrup of water and sugar, add fruit, and cook gently until fruit is tender and clear. Cool rapidly. Pack in sterilized jars, process five minutes in boiling water, and seal.

CARISSA SYRUP

Strain the syrup left over from making preserves. Fill sterilized jars or bottles, seal or cap, and process for 10 minutes in boiling water. This syrup may be used on hot breads, in cold drinks, punch, and on waffles.

CARISSA TARTS

2½ cups carissa	¼ tsp. salt
2 cups sugar	1 cup carissa juice
1 Tbsp. melted butter	4 tart shells
2½ Tbsp. tapioca	(see recipe, p. 172)

Select carissa that are firm and whole, but not overripe. Cover well with water and cook until soft. Strain. Combine tapioca, sugar, salt, butter, and carissa juice. Fill pastry shells with the mixture and bake in hot oven (450°) for 15 minutes − reduce temperature to 350° and bake for 30 minutes more. Serve cold, topped with whipped cream. Serves four.

CRYSTALLIZED CARISSA

Wash the carissas. Make a syrup of two parts sugar to one part water, in sufficient quantity to cover the fruit to be crystallized. Boil the syrup until it spins a thread, then drop in the carefully washed carissas. When they have cooked until they are transparent, remove from the syrup and place on oiled paper to dry.

FROZEN CARISSAS

Wash, peel if desired, and cut in halves lengthwise or leave whole. Pack into air-tight containers and cover with a cold syrup made of equal portions of sugar and water, stirred until the sugar is dissolved. Freeze. Delicious in fresh fruit salad or as a dessert.

JELLIED CARISSA SALAD

1 Tbsp. gelatin	¼ cup sugar
¼ cup cold water	¼ tsp. salt
1¼ cups boiling carissa juice	2 Tbsp. lemon juice
or juice and pulp	1½ cups chopped celery

Soak gelatin, stir in boiling juice, sugar, salt. Cool and add lemon juice, chill till syrupy, add celery. Chill in mold.

Coconut

Mature coconuts are filled with coconut water and covered with a dry, hard husk. Nuts with little or no water should be discarded. The most difficult part of coconut preparation is the removal of the husk. This is most efficiently done with a sharp machete or a sharp hatchet with which one chops off the petiole end of the husk, thus permitting prying off the remainder of the husk in sections. Another efficient method requires planting strongly a sharpened stake, holding the nut firmly in two hands, and then bashing it repeatedly on the sharp point to segment and loosen the husk for removal.

Puncture two of the eyes of the nut with an ice pick or, better still, by rotating a thin sharp knife to rasp away the meat. Drain off the water and keep it to add to the milk. If one strikes the shell smartly at the equator of the nut with the back of a heavy knife while holding it with the eyes up, the shell will generally break into two hemispheres. It will take perhaps four or five sharp blows to do the job. The meat can then be pried from the shell with a dull knife, using skill rather than strength. The dark skin can be trimmed off with a sharp knife.

COCONUT MILK

Coconut milk is made by grating the meat across the grain or using a fine blade in a processor. Add the coconut water and ½ cup of warm water; let stand an hour, and then squeeze through a jelly bag. This milk keeps well frozen.

FREEZING COCONUT

Coconut meat grated or left in chunks, lightly sprinkled or not with sugar, can be frozen in any vapor-proof container. It will last for 1-2 years; be sure to date the packages.

COCONUT APPLE BETTY

4 cups sliced apples
1 cup soft bread crumbs
1 cup coconut shredded
4 Tbsp. butter

½ cup brown sugar,
  firmly packed
Dash of salt
½ tsp. cinnamon

Arrange 2 cups of the apples on bottom of greased baking dish. Sprinkle with ½ cup of the bread crumbs and 1/3 cup of the coconut. Combine brown sugar, salt, and cinnamon, and sprinkle half of mixture over the coconut. Dot with 2 tablespoons of the butter. Repeat. Sprinkle remaining 1/3 cup of coconut over top. Cover and bake in moderate oven (350°) 35 minutes. Uncover and bake 10 minutes longer.

COCONUT BALLS

1 cup butter or margarine
½ cup sugar
2 cups flour

1 tsp. salt
1 tsp. vanilla
1 cup grated fresh coconut

Cream shortening and sugar well, add flour, salt, vanilla, and coconut. Form in very small balls. Bake on ungreased cookie sheet until just touched with gold. Remove from sheet, roll gently in powdered sugar.

COCONUT CANDY

1½ cups brown sugar
1 Tbsp. corn syrup
½ cup coconut milk
½ tsp. vanilla

½ cup raisins, finely chopped
½ cup dates chopped
1 cup fresh grated coconut

Boil sugar, corn syrup, and coconut milk together until a small amount of syrup forms a soft ball in cold water (235°F.) Cool. Add vanilla and beat until creamy. Add fruits and coconut. Shape into a roll about 1½ inches in diameter. Wrap in waxed paper. Chill and cut in slices.

COCONUT COOKIES

½ cup shortening
½ cup white sugar
½ cup brown sugar
1 egg
1 cup enriched flour

1 tsp. baking powder
1 tsp. soda
¼ tsp. salt
1 cup rolled oats
1 cup grated fresh coconut

Cream shortening and sugars. Add egg and beat thoroughly. Sift dry ingredients together and add to the creamed mixture. Add rolled oats and coconut. Drop by teaspoonfuls on oiled cookie sheet and bake at 350° for 10 minutes or until golden brown.

COCONUT CREAM PIE

½ cup sugar
3 Tbsp. cornstarch
2 cups milk
Pinch of salt
1 baked pie shell

3 egg yolks, beaten slightly
1 Tbsp. butter
½ tsp. vanilla
⅔ cup whipped cream
¾ cup grated coconut

Combine sugar, salt and cornstarch in a saucepan. Gradually add milk and cook over moderate heat, stirring constantly. When mixture is thickened, remove from heat.

Stir small amount of milk mixture slowly into egg yolks; slowly pour back into hot milk and beat vigorously. Add butter and cook 2 minutes longer. Remove from heat and cool. Add vanilla. Pour cooled filling into baked pie shell and place in refrigerator. Just before serving, top with whipped cream and sprinkle with coconut.

COCONUT DIVINITY CAKE FROSTING

2 cups sugar
¾ cup water
¼ tsp. salt
1 Tbsp. corn syrup

2 egg whites, beaten stiffly
1 tsp. vanilla
½ cup powdered sugar
2 to 3 cups fresh grated coconut

Combine sugar, water, salt, and corn syrup and cook over low heat until mixed well and sugar is dissolved. Cover and cook three minutes or to 238°. Pour the hot syrup over the beaten egg whites, a little at a time, beating the mixture continuously. When all syrup has been beaten into the egg whites add the powdered sugar and beat well. Frost cake at once. Sprinkle grated coconut over the top of cake and press coconut into the sides.

COCONUT DULCE

1 frozen or fresh coconut
  (grated)

4 cups water
3 cups sugar

Make a syrup of sugar and water; boil until sugar is dissolved. Add shredded coconut and cook until clear and transparent. Do not stop cooking when coconut has just a creamy appearance. It should be glistening and transparent to give most satisfactory results. Pack hot into hot jars and seal immediately.

Coconut dulce is useful for cake fillings, in boiled frostings, in sauce for ice cream, with cream cheese, over fresh pineapple, in ambrosia or other fruit compotes.

COCONUT FLAN

1 can condensed milk
6 egg yolks, lightly beaten

⅓ cup sugar
1 cup grated fresh coconut

Heat baking dish in pan of hot water. Melt sugar in frying pan, stirring until light amber; pour into baking dish and cover with coconut. Add milk to boiling water; simmer three minutes. Cool. Add egg yolks. Pour over coconut. Put in pan of hot water; bake at 350° for 30 minutes.

COCONUT FRITTERS

½ cup enriched flour
½ tsp. salt
2 tsp. sugar
¼ tsp. baking powder

1 cup grated fresh coconut
⅓ cup evaporated milk
1 Tbsp. melted butter
2 eggs, separated

Sift dry ingredients together. Add coconut, milk, and butter. Beat egg yolks slightly and add to the mixture. Fold in stiffly beaten egg whites. Drop mixture by tablespoonfuls into hot deep fat (350°) and fry until golden brown. Serve with caramel or lemon sauce.

COCONUT ICE CREAM

Open a ripe coconut and save the water. Grate the coconut and put into the top of a double boiler. Add 3 cups milk and heat. Turn off heat and let stand for 10 minutes. Strain. Put the coconut milk back into the double boiler. Add the coconut water and heat to near boiling.

Sift together ¾ cup sugar, 1 tablespoon flour, and ¼ teaspoon salt. Add the hot liquid, stirring constantly. Cook for 10 minutes in double boiler; then pour over the beaten yolks of 3 eggs. Stir, cook, and chill. When mixture begins to congeal fold in a cup of whipped cream. Freeze.

COCONUT MERINGUE PIE

½ cup butter or margarine
1¼ cups sugar
3 eggs, separated

3 Tbsp. milk
1 tsp. vanilla
2½ cups grated fresh coconut

Cream butter and 1 cup sugar. Add egg yolks and beat thoroughly. Add milk and vanilla. Fold in one stiffly beaten egg white and coconut. Place in unbaked pie shell and bake at 400° for 15 minutes. Reduce temperature to 350° and bake 15 minutes longer. Cover with meringue made with the egg whites and remaining sugar. Reduce temperature to 325°. Return to the oven to brown meringue.

COCONUT ORANGE JUMBLES

¾ cup shortening
1¼ cups sugar
2 egg yolks, well beaten
1 cup shredded coconut
2½ cups cake flour

¼ tsp. salt
½ tsp. soda
¾ cup strained orange juice
Coconut and grated orange peel

Cream shortening and sugar together. Add egg yolk and coconut and beat well. Sift together flour, salt, and soda and add to the creamed mixture alternately with orange juice. After each addition beat until smooth. Drop by ½ teaspoons onto ungreased cookie sheet. Sprinkle with additional coconut and grated orange peel. Bake in hot oven (425°) 10 to 12 minutes. Makes 50 cookies.

COCONUT PIE

Line a deep 9-inch pie pan with your favorite crust. Prick all over and chill for several hours or overnight. Bake in a hot over (350⁰) for 12 to 15 minutes. Cool. For filling use:

2 Tbsp. butter, softened
1 cup sifted confectioner's
  sugar
3 eggs, separated
½ tsp. vanilla

½ cup undiluted evaporated milk
⅛ tsp. salt
2 cups freshly grated coconut
Nutmeg to taste

Cream butter, sugar, and salt. Add egg yolks, one at a time, and beat until light. Add vanilla and milk; fold in egg whites, beaten until stiff. Fold in 1½ cups of coconut. Pour into the baked crust. Sprinkle freshly grated coconut over the top, with a sprinkle of nutmeg. Bake in a moderate oven (350°) about half an hour. When filling is set it will shrink a little. Serve warm or cold.

COCONUT SPONGE CAKE

2 cups coconut milk
2 cups white sugar
3 eggs

1 two-layer sponge cake or
  1 doz. lady fingers
2 Tbsp. sugar

Heat coconut milk with sugar and boil until it forms a syrup. Let cool. Beat egg yolks and add slowly to the cool coconut syrup. Return to heat and bring to boiling point. Remove from heat and let cool. Cover bottom layer of sponge cake with half of the cold coconut syrup. Add the top layer of cake and the remaining coconut syrup.

Beat egg whites until stiff. Add 2 tablespoons of sugar. Cover top of sponge cake and brown as meringue for pie. Serve cut in wedges.

COCONUT TOFFEE

2 ripe coconuts	1 lb. sugar
Juice of 1 lime	4 tsp. water

Grate coconut meat; add sugar and water. Bring to boil; add lime juice. Cook till brown, stirring. Pour onto a greased cookie sheet to cool. Cut into pieces.

COCONUT TOFFEE BARS

½ cup shortening	½ tsp. salt
½ cup brown sugar	1 cup sifted flour

Cream shortening, salt, and sugar. Add flour and blend mixture. Spread this mixture in 8 x 12 x 2 inch pan. Bake in moderately slow oven until delicate brown (about 15 minutes). Prepare this topping:

1 cup brown sugar	½ tsp. baking powder
2 eggs well beaten	¼ tsp. salt
1 tsp. vanilla	1½ cups shredded coconut
2 Tbsp. flour	1 cup nutmeats

Add sugar and vanilla to beaten eggs, beat until foamy; then add flour, salt, baking powder, nuts, and coconut. Spread over the baked mixture. Return to oven and bake 25 minutes. Cool and cut in small rectangles.

HAUPIA

3 coconuts	4 Tbsp. sugar
4 Tbsp. cornstarch	Pinch of salt

Grate coconut and let stand in coconut water for one hour in a warm place. Squeeze out liquid through a cloth. Put in a double boiler, add sugar and salt. When warm, add starch mixed with a little coconut water. Cook until thick, stirring constantly. Pour into shallow pan and put in refrigerator. When firm, cut in squares and serve.

HAWAIIAN CURRY

2 cups grated fresh coconut	½ cup softened butter or
3 cups milk	margarine
2 cloves garlic, chopped	½ cup flour
1 Tbsp. chopped ginger root	½ tsp. salt
2 medium onions, chopped	½ cup cream
2 apples, cored and diced	2½ cups chicken, shrimp, or
2 Tbsp. curry powder	other meat

Combine coconut and milk and bring to simmering temperature. Add garlic, ginger, onions, and apples. Blend curry powder and 2 Tbsp. of the butter. Add to the coconut mixture and cook slowly for 3 hours, stirring occasionally. Remove from heat and let stand in a cool place for several hours. Strain; blend flour with the remaining butter and add to the strained mixture. Cook, stirring constantly until thickened. Add salt and cream. Add meat or fish and continue to cook over low heat for 30 minutes. Serve with rice and the following: crisp chopped bacon, chutney, pickles, grated coconut, sliced lemon, chopped nuts, or sliced hard cooked eggs.

HOT COCONUT BREAD

Grated meat, one fresh coconut	1 cup sugar
2 eggs	2¼ cups flour
½ cup shortening	1 Tbsp. baking powder
2 cups milk or cream	

Mix first 5 ingredients together; then stir in flour and baking powder. Heat until well mixed. Pour into greased pan; bake at 325° until brown (about 40 minutes).

JAPANESE FRUIT CAKE

1 cup butter	4 eggs
2 cups sugar	1 tsp. baking powder
3¼ cups pastry flour	1 tsp. vanilla
1 scant cup water or milk	¾ cup raisins

Mix as for any cake. Divide batter into two parts. Bake first half in greased cake pan. Into the second half of the batter put one teaspoon each of cinnamon and allspice, ½ teaspoon cloves, ¾ cup raisins, chopped fine. Bake in greased cake pan.

Filling:

2 lemons, grated rind and juice	2 cups sugar
2 cups grated coconut	2 Tbsp. cornstarch
1 cup chopped nuts	1 cup boiling water

Mix all ingredients except hot water in a saucepan. Add the hot water and cook, stirring constantly. The mixture will drop from a spoon as a lump when it is done. Cool and spread between cake layers. Top with favorite icing.

MAGIC MACAROONS

⅔ cup condensed milk

3 cups shredded coconut
1 tsp. vanilla

Mix condensed milk, coconut, and vanilla. Drop by teaspoonfuld on well-greased baking sheet, about 1 inch apart. Bake in moderate oven (350°) 8 to 10 minutes or until delicate brown. Remove from pan at once.

MAGIC "SIX-WAY" COOKIES

1⅓ cups (15 oz. can)
condensed milk

½ cup peanut butter

Any one of these ingredients:

2 cups raisins
2 cups corn flakes
3 cups shredded coconut

2 cups bran flakes
1 cup chopped nut meats
2 cups chopped dates

Mix condensed milk, peanut butter, and any one of the six ingredients listed above. Drop by teaspoonfuls onto well-greased baking sheet. Bake in moderate oven (375°) for 12 minutes, or until brown. Remove from pan at once.

ORANGE COCONUT BREAD

3 cups flour
4 tsp. baking powder
1 tsp. salt
1 cup sugar
1 egg, beaten slightly

2 Tbsp. orange rind
1 cup orange juice
½ cup fresh grated coconut
⅓ cup melted shortening

Sift the flour, baking powder, salt, and sugar. Combine the orange juice, egg, orange rind, grated coconut, and melted shortening. Cool the shortening before using. Stir the liquids into the flour mixture and stir just enough to moisten. Do not overmix. Pour into a greased loaf pan and bake in a moderate oven (350°) for one hour or until done. Remove from pan. Cool. The bread will slice better the second day. Wrap in wax paper to store. Serve with softened cream cheese.

Dovyalis

The fruits of the Ceylon gooseberry *(Dovyalis hebecarpa)* are about an inch in diameter, globular with a reddish-purple velvety skin covering an acid purplish pulp containing many seeds. A closely related species, *D. abyssinica,* and some hybrids produce larger fruits with less seeds. Little used as fresh fruit, dovyalis makes good jellies, jams, and conserves.

DOVYALIS BUTTER WITH NUTS

6 cups dovyalis puree	1 cup chopped almonds
6 cups sugar	or walnuts

To make puree place fruit in saucepan with one inch of water. Cook, mashing from time to time until the fruit falls apart. Put through sieve.

Place equal quantities of dovyalis puree and sugar into saucepan and cook, stirring constantly until thick. Add nuts and continue cooking until wooden spoon stands upright in the butter. Place in jars immediately and process in water bath for 10 minutes.

DOVYALIS CATSUP

4 cups dovyalis puree	¼ cup tarragon vinegar
1 Tbsp. ginger	1 Tbsp. salt
1 Tbsp. peppercorns	1 Tbsp. molasses
½ tsp. cloves	1½ cups chopped onion
1 Tbsp. cinnamon	1 bell pepper, chopped
1 Tbsp. turmeric	1 cup celery, chopped

Cook all ingredients down to desired thickness.

Add: ½ cup brown sugar	1 cup white sugar

Cook 30 minutes more. Seal in hot, sterile jars.

DOVYALIS DELIGHT

16 whole dovyalis fruits	½ cup sugar
1½ large bananas	1 envelope plain gelatin
¼ cup Karo syrup	Whipped cream

Blend first four ingredients until liquified, making about three cups. Dissolve gelatin in dovyalis mixture and stir. Pour into mold and refrigerate until set. Serve with whipped cream.

DOVYALIS JAM

1 cup dovyalis puree   1 cup of sugar

Cook slowly in thick-bottom pan until a spoonful put on cold water holds shape.
   If a spiced product is desired, for each cup of pulp use:

¼ tsp. ground cloves   ¼ tsp. nutmeg
½ tsp. cinnamon

DOVYALIS JELLY

2 cups dovyalis juice   ¼ cup liquid pectin
3½ cups sugar

Prepare juice as directed in dovyalis juice recipe. Bring juice to boiling. Add sugar and pectin. Bring to rolling boil, stirring constantly. Cook to jelly point. Remove from heat; skim and pour into sterilized glasses.

DOVYALIS JEWELS

1 cup dovyalis puree   1½ cups chopped nuts and/or
5 Tbsp. gelatin   grated coconut
1½ cups water   3 cups sugar

Soak gelatin in ½ cup water. Boil sugar with ½ cup water. Add gelatin to syrup and boil 15 to 20 minutes, stirring constantly. Add dovyalis puree with ½ cup water. Cool. Add nuts or coconut. Pour into oiled pan, 14 x 9 in. Let stand 24 hours, cut into squares with wet knife. May be rolled in nuts or coconut. Or, pour to depth of ¼ inch in several pans, cook until set, and spread with melted white chocolate. Or, cut in small cubes, mix with whipped dessert topping, and spread between and on top of cake layers.

DOVYALIS JUICE

4 cups dovyalis   1½ cups water

Wash dovyalis and crush in bottom of kettle. Add water; bring to boiling point and simmer 10-15 minutes or until tender. For a clear juice turn into jelly bag and let drain, shifting pulp occasionally to keep juice flowing.

Fig

Mature fruit are pear shaped and vary in size, depending on the variety. They are hollow, succulent receptacles with many ovaries on their inner surfaces with or without seeds, again depending on the variety. Most species are delicious eaten fresh.

CANNED FIGS

2 cups sugar   4 cups water

Wash, sort, and clip stems from figs. Prepare enough sugar and water syrup to cover fruit. Add figs to syrup and simmer until figs look clear (about 1½ hours). Cook gently to keep fruit from breaking. Let stand overnight to "plump."

Pack into clean hot jars. Bring syrup to a boil and pour over figs. Wipe mouth of jar and seal. Process in a boiling water-bath with water to cover jars. Process pints 10 minutes, quarts 15 minutes.

FESTIVE FIG CONSERVE

2 lbs. fresh figs or   Pulp and thinly-sliced or finely
  1 qt. processed figs   ground peel of 1 orange
Juice of 1 lemon   ½ lb. raisins
1½ lbs. sugar (3 cups)   ½ cup finely chopped pecans

Cut fresh or canned figs and raisins in small pieces. Combine all ingredients except nuts, and cook until thick and transparent (about 1 hour). Add nuts 5 minutes before removing from heat. Pack in hot standard canning jars. Adjust lids. Process in a boiling water-bath canner (212°) pints, 10 minutes; quarts, 15 minutes. Serve with holiday turkey or ham.

FIG-LYCHEE COCKTAIL

3 cups peeled and cubed figs   2 Tbsp. lemon juice
1½ cups shelled lychees   ½ cup lychee juice
                                      Sugar to taste

Prepare figs. Cut lychees into quarters. Combine all ingredients and chill for 1 hour before serving in cocktail glasses.

FIG FILLING FOR CAKE

2 cups diced figs   ⅔ cup sugar
⅔ cup water   2½ Tbsp. lemon juice

Cook figs and water together until figs are soft enough to mash. Add sugar and lemon juice, and cook until mixture is thick enough to spread. Cool and spread between layers of yellow or white cake.

FIG ICE CREAM

4 cups whole milk   1 Tbsp. vanilla
1 can evaporated milk   2 Tbsp. flour
1¾ cup sugar   2 eggs, beaten
¼ tsp. salt   4 cups peeled, crushed figs

Peel and crush figs.

Mix sugar, salt and flour. Add eggs. Mix. Add to 2 cups milk; cook on low heat until thick. Stir constantly. Add 2 remaining cups milk and the evaporated milk. Blend. Add figs and vanilla. Pour into 2 ice trays, cover with wax paper. Freeze in refrigerator.

Beat, when frozen, to a smooth texture; return to trays. Cover with wax paper. Freeze until serving time.

FIG MOUSSE

2 cups peeled crushed figs   ¾ cup hot water
3 Tbsp. lime juice   1 envelope plain gelatin
1 cup sugar   ¼ cup cold water
1¼ cups heavy cream

Sprinkle crushed figs with sugar and lime juice. Let stand one hour. Soak gelatin in cold water and then dissolve in hot water. Add to figs. Chill until it begins to thicken. Whip cream until stiff. Fold into thickened fig mixture. Pour into large mold and refrigerate until firm.

FIG PRESERVES

Cover each 2 cups of figs with 1 cup of sugar and refrigerate overnight. Add 3 slices of lemon if desired. Bring to a low boil. Cook until thick as honey (about 1 hour). Stir occasionally, taking care not to break fruit any more than necessary. Cooking in heavy aluminum will help prevent sticking. Pack in hot standard canning jars. Adjust lids. Process in a boiling water-bath canner at 212°.

FLORIDA FIG FRUIT SALAD

3 cups peeled sliced fresh figs
1 cup sliced bananas (firm ripe)
2 oranges, sectioned
¼ cup lemonade concentrate

1 cup cantaloupe balls
½ cup chopped pecans or
½ cup diced celery

Cover sliced bananas with lemonade concentrate. Combine all ingredients and chill. Serve with whipped lime dressing. (For recipe, see page 91). Garnish with ripe fig.

FROZEN FIGS

Use tree-ripened figs; wash and remove stems. Figs may be left whole or cut up. They retain more of their natural juice, hence their flavor, if frozen in light sugar syrup. Use a syrup made of twice the amount of water as sugar. If desired, 1 tablespoon of lime juice per cup of water can be added. Pack figs tightly in appropriate freezer containers and cover with syrup, leaving an inch of head space; seal and freeze.

OLD-FASHIONED FIG JAM

Wash one quart figs, drain, and clip off stems. Add two cups sugar and mash. Cook slowly. Using a thermometer, remove from heat when 220° is reached. Pack into clean, hot, sterile jars.

PICKLED FIGS

4 lb. ripe figs
Whole cloves
4 cups sugar

2 cups water
4 2-inch sticks cinnamon
2 cups vinegar

Wash figs and stick each one with one or two cloves. Cook sugar, vinegar, water, and cinnamon together until syrup is fairly thick (about 10 minutes). Add figs and cook slowly until tender (about 1 hour). Place figs in hot sterilized jars, cover with boiling syrup, and seal.

REFRIGERATED FRESH PLUMPED FIGS

1 cup sugar

3 cups water

Heat the syrup to 212°. Add figs and simmer for 10 minutes. Remove from heat and let fruit stand for 10 minutes. Cool and drain well. Figs will keep for approximately a week in refrigerator.

Grumichama

The dark crimson, ½ to 1 inch, roundish, thin-skinned fruits have a soft melting flesh with a pleasant sweet flavor. They are eaten out of hand or used to make jam or jelly.

GRUMICHAMA COFFEE CAKE

Use recipe for Jaboticaba Coffee Cake, page 73, and substitute grumichama pulp in place of the jaboticabas. To prepare pulp, wash and crush the fruit, add a cup of water, cover, and bring to a boil. Simmer about 10 minutes. Then push it through a sieve or through a food mill to extract the seeds.

GRUMICHAMA JAM

3 cups pulp   2 Tbsp. lime juice
3 cups sugar

Prepare grumichama pulp as given above in Grumichama Coffee Cake. Next, add the sugar and lime juice to the pulp and cook slowly until a spoonful of the mixture will hold its shape. Place in sterilized jars and seal.

GRUMICHAMA JELLY

5 cups grumichama juice   7 cups sugar
  (about 3 qts. grumichamas)   ½ bottle liquid pectin

Sort, wash, and crush ripe grumichamas. Add 1 cup water. Cover and bring to a boil. Simmer about 10 minutes. Extract juice by draining through a jelly bag. Measure juice and put into large kettle. Bring to a boil. Remove from heat and stir in sugar. Bring to a hard boil and boil one minute. Remove from heat, skim foam, and pour into hot sterilized jars and seal.

GRUMICHAMA LIQUEUR

1 bottle brandy   1 lb. grumichamas (pitted)
1 lb. sugar

Place in an air-tight jar and invert daily for a few weeks until the sugar has dissolved, then occasionally. In about six months the fruited liqueur should be ready to use over tart fruits in desserts, or spooned over ice cream.

◁ GRUMICHAMA   69

Guava

There are varieties with fruit round, ovoid to pear-shaped, weighing up to one pound. Skin is usually yellow, but the flesh may be white, yellow, pink, or red. Fruit ranges from thin-to thick-skinned, and from few to many seeded. The best varieties have few seeds and generous firm pulp. Flavors go from sweet to acid while the distinctive aroma may be mild and pleasant or strong and penetrating.

ALOHA PUNCH

2 cups sugar
4 cups water
2⅔ cups guava juice
2⅔ cups orange juice

1⅓ cup lemon juice
1⅓ cup shredded pineapple
Grated rinds of 1 orange
   and 1 lemon
Drops of red coloring

Boil sugar and water for 3 minutes. Cool and add fruit juice and pineapple. Add all other ingredients and pour over cracked ice.

GUAVA BROWN BETTY

1 cup sugar
¼ tsp. each cinnamon
   and nutmeg
2 cups bread crumbs
¼ cup butter
1 tsp. grated lemon rind

¼ cup water
3 Tbsp. lemon, lime or
   calamondin juice
2 cups guavas, seeded and
   cut in small pieces

Blend the sugar, spices, and lemon rind. Mix crumbs and butter slightly with fork. Cover bottom of buttered pudding dish with crumbs and add ½ of the guavas. Sprinkle with the sugar mixture; repeat, cover with remaining crumbs. Mix the water, lemon juice, and pour over. Dot with butter and bake in a moderate oven (350°) for 45 minutes. Cover at first to keep crumbs from browning. Serve with cream and sugar.

GUAVA BUTTER

8 cups cooked guava pulp
6 cups sugar
¾ tsp. ground allspice

6 Tbsp. lemon juice
3 Tbsp. grated fresh ginger root
¾ tsp. ground cinnamon

Press guava pulp through a sieve before measuring the quantity. Add remaining ingredients. Cook slowly until thick, stirring frequently to prevent burning. Pour into hot, sterilized jars.

GUAVA DELIGHT

1 tsp. gelatin
2 Tbsp. cold water
3 Tbsp. boiling water
½ cup sugar

1 cup guava puree
1 Tbsp. lemon or lime juice
2 cups cream

Soak gelatin in cold water, then stir in boiling water. Add sugar, lemon or lime juice, and the guava puree. Stir until sugar is completely dissolved. Chill until thickened. Whip cream and fold into guava mixture. This may be served chilled or frozen. Garnish with fresh grated coconut.

GUAVA JAM

8 cups cooked sieved guavas
Grated rinds of 2 lemons

8 cups sugar
¼ cup lemon juice

Combine fruit and cook until most of water has evaporated. Add sugar and lemon and cook until thick. Pour into sterile jars. Seal.

GUAVA JAM CAKE

1 cup brown sugar
½ cup butter
1 egg
1 tsp. cinnamon
¼ tsp. cloves
2 tsp. baking powder

½ cup chopped raisins
1 cup soft guava jam
   (see recipe above)
1 tsp. soda
2 cups flour (whole wheat
   flour may be used)

Combine ingredients in order listed. Bake at 350° about 40 minutes.

GUAVA JELLY

4 cups guava juice

4 to 4½ cups sugar

Choose half-ripe guavas and prepare guava juice (see recipe below). Place juice in kettle and heat 5 to 10 minutes. Add sugar and bring quickly to boiling point, removing scum. Boil vigorously about 15 minutes. Test for jelly stage and then pour into sterilized glasses.

GUAVA JUICE

Wash, remove blossom end, and cut two quarts guavas into slices. Add water to cover, bring to boiling point. Boil gently for 15 minutes. Strain through a jelly bag. Heat to boiling point, pour into sterile jars and seal.

GUAVA MILK SHERBET

2¼ cups guava juice
1⅛ cups sugar
2 Tbsp. lemon or
   1½ Tbsp. lime juice

1¼ cups thin cream or
   evaporated milk
2 egg whites
1/16 tsp. salt

Boil 1 cup guava juice and 1 cup sugar together for 3 minutes. Cool and add the remaining guava and lemon juice. Place this mixture in refrigerator tray and allow it to freeze. Remove the guava mixture to a chilled mixing bowl and beat with an egg beater until the mixture is fluffy. Add the cream and fold in the stiffly beaten egg whites to which the salt and 1/8 cup sugar has been added. Pour the sherbet into the refrigerator tray and freeze.

GUAVA PUDDING

4 cups guavas, peeled, cut in
   quarters, seeds removed
Juice, 1 orange
2 tsp. lemon juice or lime

½ cup brown sugar
1 Tbsp. butter
Stale cake crumbs
1 tsp. grated orange peel

Arrange half of the prepared guavas in greased deep baking dish. Pour half of the orange and lemon juice over them; sprinkle with orange peel and sugar and dot with bits of butter. Add remainder of guavas and repeat process. Bake in a moderate oven (375°) until tender. Cover with a thin layer of cake crumbs and brown slightly in oven. Serve hot with an orange sauce.

GUAVA SAUCE CAKE

1 cup unsweetened guava pulp
1¼ cups sugar
½ cup shortening
1 egg
1¾ cups flour
¼ tsp. salt

1 tsp. soda
1 tsp. cinnamon
½ tsp. cloves
½ cup raisins
½ cup chopped nuts

Measure ¼ cup sugar and add to guava pulp. Heat to boiling point and cool. Cream shortening and remaining sugar (1 cup). Add egg and beat thoroughly. Sift together flour, salt, soda, and spices and blend some with raisins and nuts. Add remaining sifted flour to cream mixture; the raisins and nuts. Add guava pulp and beat until smooth. Pour into an oiled 8-inch square cake pan and bake at 350° for 35-40 minutes. Serve warm, plain, or with ice cream.

GUAVA SHELLS

Guavas, peeled and cut in halves	1 cup sugar
	1 cup water

Prepare guavas and remove seeds. Bring sugar and water to a boil. Drop a few of the guava halves into the boiling water. Cook about five minutes on each side. Refrigerate in leftover juice.

GUAVA SHORTCAKE

Ripe guavas	Salt
Shortcake	3 cups boiling water
3 Tbsp. cornstarch	Lemon juice
1½ cups sugar	Butter

Prepare guavas by slicing and seeding fruit. Cover liberally with sugar and let stand until sugar is dissolved. Serve between split sections of shortcake and over the top. Cover with hot sauce made from remaining ingredients. Moisten the cornstarch in a little cold water. Combine with sugar, salt, and boiling water. Stir over low heat until thickened. Remove from heat and flavor with lemon juice and butter.

GUAVA SPREADS

(1) Combine guava jelly (see recipe, page 72) and peanut butter in equal parts for sandwich spread.
(2) Mix cream cheese and guava for sandwich filling.

GUAVA TAPIOCA PUDDING

2 cups water	¼ tsp. salt
⅓ cup minute tapioca	1½ cups guava pulp
½ cup sugar	2 Tbsp. lemon juice

Cook water, tapioca, sugar, and salt until tapioca becomes clear. Cool and fold in guava pulp and lemon juice. Pour into dessert glasses and chill.

GUAVA UPSIDE-DOWN CAKE

1 cup brown sugar	2 cups diced or sliced guavas
¼ cup butter	1 box cake mix

Spread brown sugar in buttered pan. Add butter and guavas. Prepare cake mix and pour over guavas. Bake at 350°. Serve upside-down.

Jaboticaba

Grapelike in appearance with thicker and tougher dark maroon-to-black skin, this fruit is about one inch in diameter. It contains a whitish, gelatinous, subacid pulp. Each fruit contains 1 to 4 seeds and has a pleasant grapelike flavor. The fruit is good fresh or used for jams, jellies, or juice, all of which freeze well.

JABOTICABA COFFEE CAKE

1 qt. jaboticabas
2 Key limes
2 cups Bisquick or equivalent
1 cup sugar
3 Tbsp. cornstarch

Remove pits from fruit; simmer seeds in small amount of water for 10 minutes. Let stand in water overnight and then add to fruit after straining out pits. To the fruit add the lime juice, sugar, and cornstarch. Cook until thickened and then cool.

Prepare dough from coffee cake recipe on Bisquick box, or equivalent. Recipe makes four 6" x 9" shallow aluminum trays of cake. Grease trays. Spread dough about 3/8" thick over sides and bottom of trays. Fill center trough with fruit mix. Bake at 400° for 20 minutes.

JABOTICABA JAM I

Wash fruit and cut each one in half. Squeeze pulp in one pan; put skins in another pan.

Add 1 cup of water to pulp, bring to boil, and simmer 5 minutes. Pour through a wire strainer. Press with wooden spoon until most of pulp is removed from seeds. Add pulp to skins.

Measure one cup of sugar to one cup of fruit. Cook slowly at low temperature until consistency desired. Store in sterilized jars.

JABOTICABA JAM II

3 cups pulp
3 cups sugar
2 Tbsp. lime juice

Use fresh pulp or that which has been left over from jelly making. Remove seeds and put pulp through a food chopper. Fresh fruit must be cooked until tender. Add sugar and cook slowly until a spoonful of the mixture will hold its shape.

If a spiced jam is desired, for each cup of pulp add ¼ teaspoon ground cloves, ½ teaspoon cinnamon, and ¼ teaspoon nutmeg.

JABOTICABA JELLY I

4 cups jaboticaba juice
  (see recipe below)
7 cups sugar

½ bottle liquid pectin
½ cup lime juice

Bring juice to a boil. Add sugar and lime juice. Bring to a rolling boil for one minute, stirring constantly. Stir in pectin and boil one minute. Remove from heat, skim and pour into sterilized glasses. Seal.

JABOTICABA JELLY II

5 cups jaboticaba juice
  (see recipe below)

½ cup lemon or lime juice
3¾ cups sugar

Put juices and sugar into a large saucepan. Boil until jelly stage is reached (220°). Remove from fire. Let stand two minutes. Skim. Pour into sterilized jars. Seal.

JABOTICABA JUICE

Wash jaboticabas and add water to almost cover. Bring to boiling point and simmer 15 minutes. Let stand overnight. Then mash fruit and heat to boiling. Pour into jelly bag and drain for 6 hours.

JABOTICABA SYRUP

Remove seeds and skins from jaboticabas, puree pulp and measure 2 cups. Add ½ cup sugar and bring to a boil. Mix 2 Tbsp. cornstarch with 2 Tbsp. water and add slowly to pulp. Cook until transparent and use immediately for pancakes. Also delicious cooled and used over ice cream.

MANGO AND JABOTICABA PUDDING CAKE

5-6 mangos
1 cup jaboticaba juice
  (see recipe above)
½ cup brown sugar
½ cup white sugar

2 Tbsp. tapioca
Cold water
¼ stick butter or margarine, melted
1 box yellow or white cake mix
1 cup chopped pecans

Peel and slice mangos. Add jaboticaba juice, brown and white sugar and tapioca (soaked in cold water 5 minutes). Pour into 9 x 12 in. greased pan. Pour dry cake mix (no liquids) in mango mixture. Sprinkle nuts over top and dot with butter. Bake 45 minutes at 350°. Serve with ice cream or whipped topping.

Jakfruit

These giant fruits are oval to oblong and generally vary in weight from 10 to 40 pounds; some go to 110 pounds. The rind is made up of hexagonal fleshy spines. The flesh is comprised of whitish, slippery, juicy seed coverings packed together, each containing one large seed. These seed coverings have a pungent odor and a sweet or acid flavor. The fruit is good eaten raw and used in curries. The large seeds, after boiling and roasting, resemble chestnuts.

GINATAN

6 jakfruit arils, seeds removed	1 cup sugar
3 Tbsp. tapioca	4 cooking bananas (plantains)
Water	1 lb. taro
3 cups coconut cream, or	1 lb. sweet potatoes
coconut milk (see recipe, p. 52)	1 lb. yams

Place tapioca in boiling water and cook over medium heat until transparent, stirring gently from time to time. Pour off the hot water and immerse the tapioca in cold water. Leave to cool and then drain off the water.

Add sugar to the coconut cream, or milk, and bring to boil in saucepan. Peel the bananas and slice crossways. Peel and dice two yams and sweet potatoes. Cut jakfruit into strips. Add each ingredient to the boiling mixture. Cook over medium heat, stirring occasionally, until the vegetables are almost cooked. At this stage add the drained tapioca. When the mixture is completely cooked, add the remaining cup of coconut cream. Serve either hot or cold.

INDONESIAN JAKFRUIT

Peel and slice into 1½ slices, immature jakfruit, seeds and all. Then cut each circle into half.

Blend the following until smooth:

5 kimiri nuts	6 cloves garlic
2 large onions	2-4 Tbsp. sugar
1 Tbsp. coriander	Coconut milk, enough to blend
2 tsp. salt	easily (see recipe page 52)

In cooking pan, make layers of the following, starting with beans and cabbage:

Whole green beans and cabbage cut into 1-inch pieces	Pieces of cut-up chicken and pork chops or hocks
Jakfruit slices	Bay leaves
Shelled hardboiled eggs	Laos powder

Spread 1/3 of blended mixture on each layer of beans and cabbage. Sprinkle about ½ tsp. laos powder and add a bay leaf or two over the blended mixture before adding the next jakfruit layer. Pour enough coconut milk (or whole milk) to be barely seen under top layer of vegetables. Cover whole with leaves of cabbage. Cover pot and bring to a boil. Simmer several hours, adding milk as needed along with a little sugar, salt, and coriander. In 12-14 hours this dish will be dark and fairly dry and ready to eat.

JAKFRUIT APPLE MARMALADE

Ripe but firm jakfruit	Sugar
Apple pulp	

Cut and skin the jakfruit. Choose arils of about the same size, cut the end from each, and remove seed. Finely slice arils. For each 2 cups of sliced arils, use 1 cup of apple pulp and 3 cups of sugar. Mix all ingredients and cook until mixture thickens and marmalade sets. Seal in sterilized jars.

JAKFRUIT CANDY

1 ripe but firm jakfruit	1 Tbsp. lime juice
Water	Sugar

Cut jakfruit and remove skin. Choose arils about the same size, cut ends, and remove seeds. Slice large arils but leave small ones whole.

Dilute lime juice in 1 gallon of water and soak jakfruit in lime-water for 2 hours. Remove, wash, and blanch arils in boiling water for 2 minutes. Dip them immediately into cold water and drain. Make a syrup of 2 parts sugar with 1 part water. Boil arils in this syrup for 5 minutes. Leave them in syrup for 1 week. Each day remove the arils and boil syrup for 5 minutes. After the week, remove them and boil the syrup as usual. Then add them to the boiling syrup and stir gently until all water has evaporated. Remove any excess sugar from arils and, when dry, wrap each one in waxed paper. Store in sealed jars.

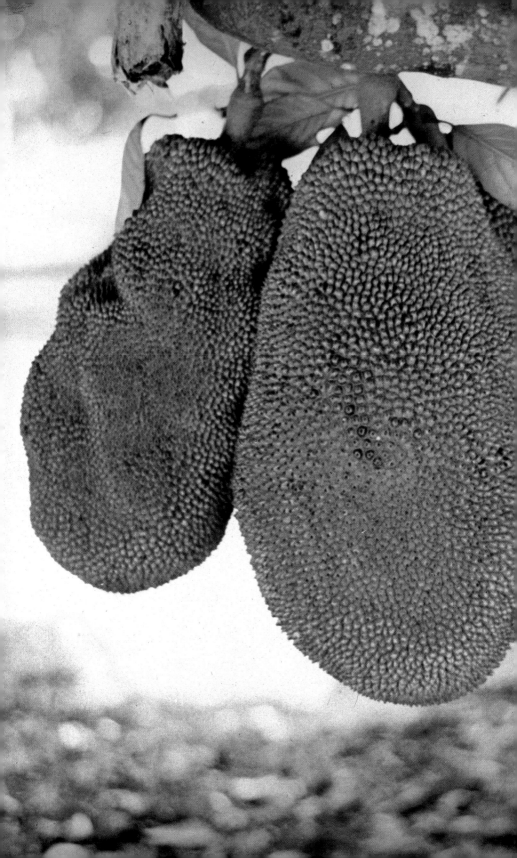

JAKFRUIT CURRY

3 cups chopped jakfruit
1 tsp. salt
1½ tsp. brown sugar
½ tsp. hot pepper powder
1 Tbsp. fresh grated coconut

2 Tbsp. cooking oil
½ tsp. mustard seeds
1 small whole red pepper
  (broken into 2 to 3 pieces)
1 tsp. lentils

Choose jakfruit that is not quite mature. Cut the fruit into 4 pieces lengthwise. Peel the thick skin off and remove the middle portion. Then cut into small cubes. Soak in cold water for 15 minutes. Drain.

On medium heat, cook the fruit with a little water, salt, brown sugar and pepper powder until tender (about ½ hour). Stir occasionally. Then add coconut gratings.

Place oil, pepper pieces, mustard seeds, and lentils in a frying pan on moderate heat. When the mustard seeds start cracking, add the cooked fruit. Mix well and remove from the heat.

JAKFRUIT PINEAPPLE MARMALADE

Ripe, firm jakfruits
Chopped pineapple

Sugar
Glucose

Cut and skin the jakfruits and remove seeds. Finely slice arils. For each cup of sliced arils, use 3 cups of pineapple, 2 cups of sugar, and ½ cup glucose. Mix all ingredients in pan and cook until the mixture thickens and marmalade satisfies the testing. Seal in sterilized jars.

JAKFRUIT WITH CRABS

Unripe jakfruit
4 medium soft-shelled crabs
½ cup chopped onion

1 Tbsp. chopped ginger
3 cups coconut cream, or milk
3 medium, sliced tomatoes

Wash jakfruit and chop into small pieces. Wash and cut crabs into halves. Measure 6 cups of jakfruit into a saucepan and add all ingredients, including crabs, with salt to taste. Cook over medium heat, fairly slowly, until the mixture produces oil. Serve hot with rice.

STUFFED JAKFRUIT

Cut fruit in half. Oil hands with vegetable oil and remove each aril. Remove seeds. Using broken pieces of arils, add sufficient white raisins, coconut, and nuts (pecans or almonds) to stuff arils. Put through food chopper and stuff individual arils. Serve chilled, 2 or 3 per person.

Jambolan (Java Plum)

These shiny, dark-purple to black fruits are up to 1½ inches long. Each contains a single large oblong seed surrounded by a thin layer of yellowish pulp. The pulp is juicy and acid but often has an undesirable astringent taste. The astringency can be reduced by soaking the plums in salt water before cooking. Excellent wine can be made from these plums. Remove the seeds by pushing them through a hole in a thin board which is sized to strip off the pulp.

JAMBOLAN JELLY

1¾ cups jambolan juice
1¼ cups water
½ cup lemon or lime juice

7 cups sugar
½ cup liquid pectin

The plum contains little or no pectin, so it is necessary to combine the juice with fruit of a high pectin content, or to use commercial pectin, in order to make jelly.

Combine water and plum juice; bring to boil. Add sugar and heat to boiling quickly; add pectin, stirring constantly. Allow to come to a brisk roll and boil vigorously for one minute. Remove from heat, skim, and pour quickly into hot sterilized jars. Seal.

JAMBOLAN JUICE

8 cups firm ripe plums

1¼ cups water

Wash plums and remove stems. Place in saucepan with water and cook until fruit is soft (20 to 25 minutes). Pour into thick jelly bag and allow juice to drain. Pour off clear liquid for jelly.

Juice sweetened with sugar can be put into jars and processed for five minutes just below boiling. This juice can be used in making punch or jelly.

JAMBOLAN PRESERVES

4 cups fruit
4 cups sugar

2 Tbsp. lime juice

Wash and cut pulp from seeds. Do not peel. Bring fruit, sugar, and lime juice to a boil. After boiling 20 minutes remove, pour into hot sterilized jars, and seal. Boil in hot water bath 5 minutes to insure keeping.

Kumquat

The kumquat, smallest member of the citrus family, bears early and abundantly. The fruits, round or elongated, are orange, attractive, and aromatic. The skin is spicy and the flesh delightfully acid. It is the only citrus fruit which is eaten, skin and all.

BAKED KUMQUATS

Parboil well-washed kumquats for 5 minutes. Drain and cool. Remove a slice from the top of each kumquat. Remove center from each and fill the depression with sugar. Stand kumquats upright close together in a shallow, buttered pan. Pour pineapple juice over them. Bake in a moderate oven 15 minutes. Use as a garnish.

CANDIED KUMQUATS

2 cups fresh kumquats	1 cup water
2 cups sugar	Pecan halves

Stem and wash kumquats. Cover with water and boil 5 minutes, drain, and cut into halves, lengthwise. Combine sugar and water and bring to a boil. Drop in kumquats and cook over low heat 10 minutes. Put into a bowl for overnight. Next day cook 20 minutes. Lift from syrup and put on wax paper to cool. Press a pecan on each piece and roll in sugar.

KUMQUAT BUTTER

Wash and scrape kumquats. Cut in half and take out seeds. Run halves through food chopper, using medium blade. For each cup kumquats add ½ cup sugar. Let stand 2 hours. Pour into saucepan and cook until clear. Pour into small jars. Seal and simmer for 10 minutes in water.

KUMQUAT CONSERVE

Use recipe for Kumquat Butter, above, except use ¾ cup sugar, ½ cup raisins, and ½ cup nutmeats for each cup of ground fruit.

KUMQUAT JAM

Wash and scrape kumquats. Cut in halves and remove seeds. Chop to medium size. Measure and add 1 cup of sugar and ½ cup of water for each cup of kumquats. Let stand one hour. Pour into saucepan and cook rapidly until thickened. Pour into sterilized glasses and seal.

KUMQUAT JELLY

4 cups kumquats   3 cups water
2 cups sugar

Wash kumquats, clean thoroughly, and cut in slices. Add water. Boil for 15 minutes. Cover and let stand overnight. Boil again for five minutes. Remove from heat and drip through a flannel bag.

Place juice in a large saucepan, add sugar, and boil to jelly stage. Remove from sire, skim, and pour into sterilized jars and seal.

KUMQUAT PRESERVES

2 cups kumquats   1 stick cinnamon
1 cup water   1 lime (sliced thinly)
2 cups sugar

Cut small crosswise gash in each kumquat. Cover fruit with water and bring to a boil. Drain. Bring sugar and water to a boil, drop in kumquats, cinnamon, and lime and cook 10 minutes. Let stand overnight. Cook uncovered for 10 minutes; let stand until cool. Bring to a boil and cook until fruit is clear and syrup thick. Pack into sterilized jars while hot; cover with hot syrup and seal at once.

KUMQUAT RELISH

To the recipe for Kumquat Conserve (see recipe, page 84) add ¼ cup vinegar or lime juice, 1 cup chopped celery, 1/3 cup chopped onions, 1 cup chopped green or red sweet peppers. Add spices to taste.

SPICED KUMQUATS

4 cups kumquats   2 small pieces ginger root
½ Tbsp. mace   1 cup fruit vinegar
1 stick cinnamon   ½ tsp. allspice
1½ cups sugar   ½ cup water
½ tsp. whole cloves   Soda

Clean fruit by washing thoroughly. Sprinkle with soda, using 1 Tbsp. to 1 quart of kumquats. Cover with boiling water, let stand 10 minutes. Pour water off and rinse thoroughly in 3 changes of water.

Make a ½-inch slit in each fruit. Cover with water and boil gently until almost done. In separate pan, boil sugar and spices (tied in a bag). Drain kumquats and drop into syrup. Boil 10 minutes and remove spice bag. Cook until fruit is transparent. Pack in sterilized jars.

Lime

There are two major species of limes produced commercially in south Florida. The Mexican or true lime *(Citrus aurantifolia)* known as 'Mexican,' 'West Indian,' or 'Key' lime, and the Tahiti lime *(C. latifolia)* also known as 'Persian' or 'Bearss.' Fruit of both are best used before fully mature and yellow. They are prized for the refreshing flavor in drinks and in cooking. For most recipes either of the limes can be used, although the Key Lime has its own unique flavor.

FROZEN LIME DESSERT

3 Tbsp. butter, melted	¼ cup sugar
1 cup fine graham cracker crumbs	1 Tbsp. grated lime rind
2 eggs, separated	⅔ cup lime juice or
1 15-oz. can condensed milk	1 can (6 oz.) frozen limeade

Combine butter and graham cracker crumbs. Press 2/3 cup of crumb mixture on bottom and sides of a lightly buttered refrigerator tray; chill. Beat egg yolks until thick; combine with condensed milk. Stir in lime rind and juice; mix well. Beat egg whites until stiff; gradually add sugar until very stiff. Fold into lime-milk mixture. Turn into prepare refrigerator tray; sprinkle edge with remaining crumbs. Place in freezer and chill until firm, about 6 hours. Top with whipped cream.

KEY LIME PIE

3 eggs, separated	¾ cup Key lime juice
1 can condensed milk (15-oz.)	1 pie shell
⅓ cup sugar	

Beat egg yolks. Add condensed milk and beat again. Add lime juice and beat until smooth. Pour into pie crust. Beat egg whites to top pie with meringue and bake at 375° 5 minutes, or use whipped topping. Chill until served.

KEY LIME SLUSH

2 cups crushed ice cubes	3 Tbsp. low calorie sugar
3 large Key limes	substitute

Dissolve sugar in Key lime juice and add water to make about ¾ cup. Pour this over crushed ice in blender. Blend all ingredients until slushy. East with spoon. Practically no calories and delicious.

KEY WEST LIME PIE

6 eggs	1 can condensed milk
½ cup Key lime juice	½ to 1 cup fresh grated coconut
½ cup sugar	1 lightly browned pie shell

Beat the yolks of 4 eggs and 2 whole eggs. Reserve the whites of 4 eggs for meringue. Add the condensed milk to the egg yolk and mix well. Add lime juice, mix, and fold in the fresh coconut. Pour into pie shell and bake 5 minutes at 425°.

Beat the egg whites until foamy. Add sugar gradually and continue beating until the whites are stiff. Remove pie from oven and cover with meringue. Bake 4-5 minutes longer at 425° until meringue is golden brown.

LIME BUTTER SAUCE

½ cup butter	3 Tbsp. lime juice
¼ tsp. tabasco	

Melt butter; add lime juice and tabasco. Use as sauce for fish, seafood, or asparagus, spinach, broccoli, or green beans.

LIME CHIFFON PIE

1 envelope unflavored gelatin	1 cup sugar
¼ cup cold water	¼ tsp. salt
4 eggs, separated	½ cup heavy cream, whipped
2 tsp. grated lime rind	1 9-inch baked pastry shell
	or graham cracker crust

Soften gelatin in cold water. Combine slightly beaten egg yolks with lime rind and juice, ½ cup of the sutar, and salt. Cook in top of double boiler 10 minutes, stirring constantly. Add gelatin and stir until dissolved. Allow mixture to cool until almost firm. Beat egg whites stiff — but not dry. Add remaining ½ cup sugar slowly. Beat gelatin mixture, then fold into egg whites and whipped cream. Turn into pastry shell and chill until firm.

LIME CREAM FROSTING

1 3-oz. package cream cheese	2½ cups sifted confectioner's sugar
1 Tbsp. lime juice	1 tsp. grated lime rind

Blend cream cheese and lime juice. Add sugar gradually, blending well. Add lime rind and, if desired, a few drops of green good coloring. Mix again. Use for cake icing.

LIME DESSERT SAUCE

1 Tbsp. cornstarch
½ cup sugar
Cold water

¾ cup boiling water
2 Tbsp. butter or margarine
2½ Tbsp. lime juice

Mix cornstarch with sugar. Blend to a smooth paste with a small amount of cold water. Gradually stir paste into boiling water. Continue stirring over moderate heat until thickened. Remove from fire. Add butter and lime juice. Sauce can be served hot or cold over puddings, fruit fritters, or other desserts.

LIME FRENCH DRESSING

1 tsp. salt
1 tsp. paprika
½ tsp. mustard
½ cup salad oil

1 tsp. sugar
¼ cup grapefruit juice
¼ cup lime juice
¼ tsp. onion juice

Mix dry ingredients in small bowl. Add oil and beat with rotary beater. Add grapefruit juice, lime juice, and onion juice. Beat until well blended. Yields one cup. Store in refrigerator in covered jar. Shake well before using. This dressing is also excellent for thinning mayonnaise.

LIME MARINADE

½ cup key lime juice
⅓ cup water
1 tsp. honey
1 tsp. salt

⅛ tsp. freshly ground pepper
½ tsp. dried thyme
1 Tbsp. oil
1 clove garlic, cut into small pieces

Place all ingredients into blender and blend well.

Chicken pieces may be marinated in this baste for several hours, even overnight, or apply to chicken pieces every 15 minutes while roasting at 325° for 1½ hours.

LIME PUDDING

1 cup sugar
3 Tbsp. flour
3 Tbsp. butter
1 tsp. grated lime rind

1 cup milk
2 eggs, separated
3 Tbsp. lime juice

Combine sugar, flour and butter in a mixing bowl. Add the unbeaten egg yolks, lime juice, grated lime rind, and milk. Beat egg whites until stiff. Fold into yolk mixture. Pour into buttered 1 quart mold or 6 custard cups. Place in pan of hot water and bake 1 hour in slow oven (325°), or until the pudding leaves the sides of the baking pan (35 minutes for custard cups). The finished pudding has a cake-like top with a smooth delicious lime sauce beneath. Serve warm or cold with or without whipped cream.

LIME SHERBET OR ICE

1 envelope unflavored gelatin	1 egg white
3½ cups water	1 cup lime juice
1½ cups sugar	

Set temperature control of refrigerator for fast freezing. Sprinkle gelatin on ½ cup of the water in saucepan to soften. Place over medium heat, stirring constantly, until gelatin is dissolved. Add remaining 3 cups water, sugar, and lime juice; stir until sugar is dissolved. Pour into an 8-cup loaf pan or refrigerator trays. Place in freezing compartment of refrigerator; freeze, stirring occasionally. Break up frozen mixture in tray; add unbeaten egg white and beat with electric mixer or rotary beater just until smooth. If desired tint with few drops green food coloring. Return to freezing compartment and freeze until firm.

NOTE: For Lime Ice, omit egg white. Beat mixture until smooth and return to freezing compartment.

SPICED LIMEADE

6 large limes	1 tsp. whole cloves
½ cup sugar	Cushed ice
1 cup water	Gingerale
1 or 2 pieces stick cinnamon	

Combine sugar, water, cinnamon, and cloves. Heat until sugar is dissolved and simmer ten minutes. Remove from heat. Cool and add lime juice. Fill glasses with crushed ice. Pour lime juice to fill half of each glass. Finish filling glasses with gingerale. Garnish with sprig of mint or a slice of lime.

WHIPPED LIME DRESSING

1 3-oz. pkg. of soft cream cheese	½ cup mayonnaise dressing
2 Tbsp. lime juice	2 Tbsp. sugar

Mash cream cheese with fork. Blend in mayonnaise. Add lime juice and continue mixing. Serve over fruit salad.

Loquat

These yellow-to-orange fruits are one to two inches long, ovoid or pear-shaped with a thin, peelable, downy skin. The juicy, firm flesh is pale-yellow to orange and has a mild tart-to-sweet taste. Fruits commonly contain multiple seeds. Fresh off the tree or peeled and stewed, the fruit is very tasty. Blanched, peeled, and frozen in simple syrup, the flesh acquires a pleasant almondy flavor if the pits have not been removed.

FROZEN LOQUATS

4 pts. loquats

Syrup made from:
3½ cups sugar
3½ cups water
¾ tsp. ascorbic acid (optional)

Wash well-ripened loquats. Scald, peel, and remove seeds. Pack fruit in appropriate freezing containers and cover with syrup. Leave ½ inch headspace, seal, and freeze.

JIFFY LOQUAT RELISH

2 cups loquats
½ cup candied orange peel
½ cup candied grapefruit peel
½ cup raisins
½ tsp. cinnamon

¼ cup sugar
2 Tbsp. lemon juice
1 Tbsp. cider vinegar
2 Tbsp. candied ginger

Prepare loquats by washing and removing the blossom ends, stems, and seeds. Blanch and peel. Measure loquats and other ingredients, and blender chop until finely mixed. Refrigerate overnight in covered glass container to allow flavor to develop. Use within a week or ten days.

LOQUAT AMBROSIA

3 bananas
1 cup orange segments
½ cup grated coconut

1 cup pineapple chunks
1 cup loquat chunks
Powdered sugar

Slice bananas and cut orange segments. Combine all fruits and sugar lightly; chill. Sprinkle with coconut just before serving.

LOQUAT FRUIT SALAD

2 cups sliced fresh loquats	1 cup sliced bananas
1 cup pineapple tidbits	⅓ cup mayonnaise
1 cup orange sections	¼ cup pecans

Peel, seed, and thinly slice loquats. Combine with pineapple, orange sections, and sliced bananas. Chill about an hour. Drain off fruit juice and fold in mayonnaise. Serve on crisp lettuce leaves. Garnish with pecans.

LOQUAT GRAPE SALAD

8 to 10 loquats	1 lime
½ cup chopped pecans	1½ cups seedless grapes

Blanch and peel seedless grapes. Remove seeds and slice. In center of a lettuce leaf on each serving plate, pile some grapes and circle with loquat slices. Sprinkle with pecans and serve with mayonnaise.

LOQUAT JAM

1 qt. loquats	3 cups sugar
2 cups water	¼ cup lemon juice

Prepare loquats by washing, removing the blossom ends, stems and seeds. Peel if desired. Blender chop or put through food chopper. Combine 1 quart of fruit with 2 cups of water and cook for about 10 minutes. Stir in sugar and lemon juice and boil rapidly until the jellying point is reached (223°). Pour into hot clean ½ pint jars, leaving ½ inch headspace. Wipe jar mouths and adjust lids.

LOQUAT JAM CAKE

1 cup sugar	1 tsp. soda
¾ cup shortening	1 tsp. cloves
2 cups cake flour	1 tsp. nutmeg
3 eggs	1 tsp. allspice
1 cup loquat jam	1 tsp. cinnamon
(see recipe above)	1 cup raisins
3 Tbsp. buttermilk	1 cup chopped pecans

Cream shortening and sugar together. Add beaten eggs. Sift flour and spices together. Add soda to buttermilk. Add flour mixture to creamed mixture, alternately with milk. Cut raisins with scissors, then stir in jam, nuts, and raisins. Bake in greased loaf pan at 350° for approximately 30 minutes.

LOQUAT PIE

4 cups loquats
1 cup sugar
Unbaked pie crust

1 tsp. allspice
3 tsp. minute tapioca
3 Tbsp. butter

Peel, seed, and chop fruit. Add remaining ingredients. Pour into unbaked pie crust and cover with lattice top crust. Bake at 350° for one hour.

LOQUAT PRESERVES

1 qt. loquats
1½ cups water

1½ cups sugar

Wash and seed fruit. Remove peeling if objectionable. Dissolve sugar in water, add loquats, and cook until the fruit has a transparent look (226°). Pack into hot pint jars. Leave ½ inch headspace; adjust lids and process in boiling water-bath canner 10 minutes.

LOQUAT UPSIDE-DOWN CAKE

3 cups sliced loquats
1 cup brown sugar
½ cup raisins

1 tsp. allspice
½ tsp. salt
½ pkg. yellow cake mix

Peel, seed, and thinly slice loquats. Combine with brown sugar, raisins, allspice, and salt. Spread on well buttered 13 x 9 x 2 inch pan. Prepare yellow cake mix according to directions. Pour batter over fruit and bake in moderate oven 350° about 40 minutes. Loosen cake from sides of pan; invert on large plate and serve with or without whipped cream.

SWEET SPICED LOQUATS

2 qts. loquats
1 cup hot water
1 cup vinegar
4 cups sugar

1 Tbsp. whole cloves
2 sticks cinnamon
1 lemon sliced or
 3 calamondins sliced

Wash loquats and remove stem and blossom ends. Cut loquats lengthwise on one side to remove seeds. Steam 2-3 minutes in water to soften and to prevent shriveling. Add other ingredients (tie spices in cheesecloth bag and pound lightly) and cook gently about 10 minutes. Let stand overnight. Reheat to boiling and cook gently until syrup is somewhat thick. Pack into clean hot pint jars; adjust lids. Process in boiling water-bath canner for 5 minutes.

Lychee and Longan

These two fruits are similar in structure and are sisters. No attempt will be made to present separate recipes as either serves equally well.

The lychee ripens about a month before the longan. The lychee has a warty yellow to red leathery skin covering its 1 to 1.5 inch fruit. The edible flesh (aril), whitish, translucent, juicy with excellent subacid flavor, surrounds one large, shiny, dark brown seed. Fresh picked fruit quick frozen in polyethylene bags can be kept many months and approaches the flavor of fresh, especially if eaten before completely thawed. Lychees are best eaten fresh but do well dried whole, frozen whole, or peeled and pitted.

The longan fruit resembles the lychee in structure but is milder, less acid-flavored, externally smoother, and of a yellowish-tan to brown color. Like the lychee, the edible portion is the generally 1/4 to 1/2 inch of juicy aril between rind and large seed. Fresh fruit can be eaten right off the tree or quick frozen. Longans are also easily dried whole or peeled and pitted for stewing.

FROZEN LYCHEES

Lychees are very juicy. Their tender quality is best preserved by freezing in the shell. Leave about a quarter of an inch of stem on each fruit to protect the shell from breaking and to aid in removing the shell after thawing. For freezing they can be placed in plastic bags closed with "twistems." To prevent loss of juice, cover with sugar syrup made of one part of sugar to two parts of water. On thawing, discard the liquid and peel the fruit.

FRUIT COCKTAIL

2 cups seeded fresh lychees or longans	1 cup white grapes
2 cups pineapple tidbits	2 Tbsp. sugar
1 cup sliced bananas	2 Tbsp. lime juice

Peel and cut lychees in uniform size. Combine with other fruits. Pour off juice and stir in sugar and lime juice. Cover fruit with this mixture and chill about an hour before serving.

LYCHEE, PAPAYA AND PINEAPPLE SALAD

1 pt. lychees, slightly defrosted	⅓ cup mayonnaise
1 qt. diced pineapple and papaya	2 tsp. lemon juice

Combine the fruit and add the lemon juice. Add the mayonnaise, mix, and serve on lettuce leaves. Can be sprinkled with fresh grated coconut.

LYCHEE PARFAIT

Peel and pit half a pound of lychees; marinate them overnight in brandy. Into five parfait glasses alternate a layer of lychees, pistachio ice cream, and whipped cream until the glasses are filled. Top with whipped cream and whole, unpeeled lychees.

To make sure the cream is sufficiently stiff, fold into it lightly the stiffly beaten white of an egg. Place in a freezer until ready to serve but do not allow it to refreeze.

LYCHEE SALAD

1 cup lychees
1 cup creamed cottage cgeese
1 Tbsp. chopped preserved ginger

⅓ cup mayonnaise
½ cup shelled pecans

Peel and remove seed from lychees. Mix ginger with cottage cheese. Add 1 tablespoon mayonnaise if desired. Add lychee pulp and mix. Serve on lettuce. Garnish with grated fresh coconut.

MOLDED LYCHEE SALAD

½ pound sliced and pitted
    fresh lychees

1 pkg. lime flavored gelatin

Prepare gelatin by directions on package. When it has thickened slightly, stir in the lychees and put in refrigerator until firm. Serve on lettuce with dressing made of half whipped cream and half mayonnaise.

STUFFED LYCHEES

Remove seeds from peeled lychees and stuff with cream cheese which has been thinned with a little mayonnaise or whipped cream. Wedge a pecan half into each one for in-between-meal or midnight snack. For dessert, put three or four stuffed lychees in a small bowl, cover them generously with whipped cream, and sprinkle with finely chopped pecans.

Macadamia Nut

Culture of this nut from Australia started in the late 1800s in Hawaii. The fruit consists of a fleshy husk enclosing a spherical ½ to 1 inch hard brown shelled kernel. The shell is tough and fibrous and difficult to crack; however, softer-shelled cultivars are being grown. The nuts are one of the most delicious known, with a very high energy value averaging 9.3% protein, 78.2% fat, and 8% carbohydrate.

CHICKEN QUEEN KAPIOLANI

3½ to 4 lb. chicken	1 tsp. sugar
Salt	1 cup coarsely chopped
¼ lb. butter	macadamia nuts
1 lb. cooking apples	1 glass cider liqueur

Disjoint the chicken and sprinkle with salt. Then fry lightly in a saucepan with the butter. Place chicken and butter liquid in a glass baking dish with the peeled sliced apples. Sprinkle with the sugar and coarsely chopped macademia nuts. Add the cider liqueur. Cover the dish and set in an oven (375°). Cook until chicken is done (about 40 to 45 minutes).

COCONUT MACADAMIA CHICKEN

4 or 5 whole chicken breasts, split and boned	⅓ tsp. thyme
	⅓ tsp. monosodium glutamate
Salt	1 jar (4 oz.) sliced pimentos
Freshly ground pepper	⅔ cup golden raisins
4 Tbsp. butter	2 Tbsp. fresh lemon juice
½ cup thinly sliced green onions	¾ cup macadamia bits
1 Tbsp. brown sugar	Coconut crust (recipe below)

Season chicken pieces generously with salt and pepper. Gently brown on all sides in butter. Arrange pieces in single layer in baking dish. Add onions to the frying pan and stir to coat with drippings. Stir in brown sugar, ¼ tsp. salt, thyme, monosodium glutamate, pimentos, raisins, and lemon juice. Spoon evenly over chicken. Cover and bake at 375° for 45 minutes or until chicken is tender.

Remove cover, sprinkle coconut crust over chicken, and then sprinkle with macadamia bits. Bake uncovered for 10 minutes more. Spoon juices over chicken as it is served.

Coconut crust: Toss 5 Tbsp. melted butter, 2 Tbsp. lemon juice, ¼ tsp. salt, ¼ tsp. pepper, 1½ cups flaked coconut, and 2 Tbsp. chopped fresh parsley.

CRUMB NUT COFFEE CAKE

2 cups sifted flour
2 cups sugar
½ tsp. ground cinnamon
¼ tsp. ground nutmeg
½ cup butter

¾ cup finely chopped macadamia
  nuts
1 tsp. baking soda
¼ tsp. salt
1 cup sour cream
1 egg, beaten

Sift together in mixing bowl flour, sugar, cinnamon, and nutmeg. Cut in butter until particles are fine. Mix half this crumb mixture with ½ cup macadamia nuts and press over bottom of 9 inch square baking pan. Mix soda and salt into sour cream; add to remaining crumb mixture along with egg. Mix thoroughly. Spread batter evenly over crumbs in pan. Top with remaining macadamia nuts. Bake about 40 minutes at 350°. Cut into squares.

FRIED SHRIMP, MACADAMIA

1 lb. fresh large shrimp
1 large onion
3 whole cloves
1 whole lemon
Sprigs of parsley

Salt and pepper
2 eggs, beaten
1½ cups finely grated (like bread
  crumbs) macadamia nuts
Oil for frying

Gently boil the large shrimp for about 5 minutes in water with the onion stuck with the cloves, lemon cut in half, several sprigs of parsley, and pinch of salt and pepper. When cooked, remove the shell from the shrimp and carefully remove black line from the backs. Dip each shrimp separately in macademia nut crumbs, then in the beaten egg, and again in macademia nut crumbs. Fry until golden brown in deep fat. Drain on absorbent paper. Serve with a curry flavored mayonnaise.

FROZEN PINEAPPLE AND MACADAMIA SALAD

6-8 ozs. cream cheese
1 cup mayonnaise
1 cup whipped cream
  (unsweetened)
1 cup chopped macadamia nuts

¼ cup sugar
1 cup cubed (canned) pineapple
½ cup chopped brandy flavored
  maraschino cherries
Crisp lettuce leaves

Cream the cheese until smooth. Add mayonnaise, whipped cream and blend well. Mix in the chopped macadamia nuts, sugar, and fruits. Pack in a mold and freeze, or put in refrigerator for several hours. Serve on crisp lettuce leaves.

MACADAMIA BUTTER CRISPS

1 cup soft butter	2 cups sifted flour
1 cup sugar	1 tsp. ground nutmeg or ginger
1 egg, separated	1 cup finely chopped macadamia nuts

Cream together butter and sugar. Beat in egg yolk thoroughly. Sift flour with nutmeg (or ginger) and stir into creamed mixture. Spread in even layer over jelly roll pan (15 x 10 inches). Beat egg white slightly and brush over top. With fingertips smooth the surface. Then sprinkle macadamia nuts over dough and press in. Bake at 275° for one hour. While still hot, cut into 1½-inch squares. Cool on rack. Makes about 6 dozen.

MACADAMIA CRUSTED SOLE

½ cup soft butter	½ cup finely chopped macadamia nuts
½ cup shredded or grated Parmesan cheese	Freshly ground black pepper
4 sole fillets (about 1½ lbs.)	

Spread half of the butter over bottom of shallow baking pan. Sprinkle with half of the Parmesan. Wipe sole dry with damp cloth and arrange in a single layer over cheese. Dot sole with remaining butter and sprinkle with remaining cheese and the macadamia bits. Bake in hot oven (400°), basting occasionally with melted butter and cheese, for 15 minutes. Serve with drippings from pan spooned over fish, and sprinkle with ground pepper.

MACADAMIA NUT PIE I

3 eggs, separated	1 cup chopped macadamia nuts
1 cup sugar	1 cup crushed graham crackers
Dash of cream of tartar	1 tsp. vanilla

Beat egg whites with sugar until stiff. Add dash of cream of tartar. Then add the chopped nuts, graham crackers, and vanilla. Place all into a greased 8-inch pie tin and bake at 350° for slightly less than 20 minutes. Cool and top with whipped cream or commercial topping.

MACADAMIA NUT PIE II

3 eggs	2 Tbsp. dark rum (optional)
⅔ cup sugar	1 tsp. vanilla
1 cup light corn syrup	1 cup chopped macadamia nuts
¼ cup melted butter	Unbaked 8-inch pie crust

Beat until thoroughly mixed eggs, sugar, syrup, rum, and vanilla. Stir in the macadamia nuts. Turn into pie shell and bake at 375° for 40 to 50 minutes, just until filling is set. Cool before serving.

MAUNA LOA SALAD

6 to 8 oz. cream cheese	1 can white grapes, seedless
2 Tbsp. sugar	¼ lb. finely chopped macadamia
½ tsp. salt	nuts
Pinch cayenne pepper	2 Tbsp. gelatin
Juice of 3 lemons	2 cups water

Cream the cheese until smooth. Then add sugar, salt, cayenne, lemon juice, grapes and finely chopped macadamia nuts. Soak gelatin in a cup of water, add remaining water. Heat and set aside to cool. Pour dissolved gelatin over other mixed ingredients and stir thoroughly. Pour into a ring mold, cover and set in refrigerator until firm. Serve on lettuce leaves with mayonnaise.

NUTTED VEAL STEAK

3 Tbsp. butter	1 cup sour cream
4 veal steaks	½ cup chopped macadamia nuts
Freshly ground pepper	¼ cup dry sherry
Salt	

Melt butter in large frying pan, add steaks and saute over medium heat until tender. Season with salt and pepper lightly. Remove to warm serving platter and keep warm. Add sherry to pan and cook until slightly reduced. Turn heat to low and add sour cream and macadamia nuts to heat through, stirring to blend. Pour sauce over veal and serve.

TROPICAL SALAD

¼ to ¾ lb. fresh crab meat or 1 can (7 oz.) crab	1½ cups chopped macadamia nuts
	Crisp lettuce leaves
2 small grapefruit, peeled and cut into sections	Lemon sauce (recipe below)
1 large avocado, peeled and sliced	

Arrange crab, grapefruit, and avocado slices in lettuce leaves on chilled plates. Sprinkle with macadamia nuts. Generously spoon dressing over salad and serve.

Lemon sauce: Shake together 1 cup salad oil, ¼ cup fresh lemon juice, 1 teaspoon grated fresh lemon peel, ½ teaspoon salt, ½ teaspoon dry mustard, and ¼ teaspoon freshly ground pepper.

Malay Apple

This fruit looks like a small red apple but is pear-shaped and about 4 inches long by 3 inches wide. Thick, white, somewhat dry flesh surrounds a single large seed. It has a distinct rose odor and no distinct flavor. It may be eaten fresh and, if cooked, needs flavoring.

CANNED MALAY APPLES

Slice Malay apple in strips about 3/8 inch wide. Make a sugar syrup of one part water and one part sugar. Boil 5 minutes. Add apple strips and boil until fruit is clear, or to 220°. Remove from fire, cover, and set aside for 24 hours. Boil again to approximately 226°. Again set aside for 24 hours.

Boil the fruit for the third time to 238°. Drain. Place on racks and put into 200° oven to dry. When partially dry roll in sugar and return to oven. When dry, pack in airtight containers, seal, and refrigerate.

MALAY APPLE PIE

4 eggs, beaten slightly	1 tsp. cinnamon
1½ cups light cream	¼ tsp. cloves
1 cup sugar	1½ cups Malay apple pulp
¼ tsp. salt	½ cup fresh grated coconut
1 tsp. lemon juice	9-inch unbaked pie shell

Mix ingredients in order given. Brush pie shell with egg white. Pour pie mixture in shell. Bake ten minutes at 400° and then lower heat to 300° and bake until custard is firm.

SUKIYAKI

1 lb. steak cut in strips	2 cups mushrooms, sliced
¼ lb. green beans	1½ cups bean sprouts
2 medium onions, sliced	2 large tomatoes, quartered
3 stalks celery, sliced diagonally	Oriental noodles
2 cups spinich, stems removed	1 Tbsp. sugar
1 cup green onion tops, sliced diagonally	½ cup soy sauce
	½ cup light cream
3 large Malay apples, sliced thin	Cooked rice

Place meat and each vegetable in separate bowls. Put meat in a deep skillet that has been lightly oiled. When browned on both sides (about 4 minutes) push to one side of skillet and add and saute the vegetables placing them in sequence, beginning with those that need longer cooking. Lastly, add the bean sprouts. Vegetables should retain their crispness and good color. Then add the sugar, soy sauce, and cream. Cook for three minutes and serve over rice. Sprinkle with noodles.

Mamey Sapote

The fruit is ellipsoidal or ovoidal with a prominent point and ranges from 3 to 8 inches in length. The thick, russet-brown skin has a rough and scruffy surface. The flesh, salmon to reddish, is firm, thick, aromatic, almost free from fiber, contains a large brown seed, and can be eaten with a spoon. It is eaten out of hand or used in preserves, drinks, or a delicious sherbet. Many consider it impossible to tell from outward appearances when the fruit is ripe, as the brown exterior layer of the skin undergoes no color change upon ripening. One can either wait for the fruit to fall or scratch the surface of the skin with the fingernail on the underside of the fruit to determine the color of the flesh just beneath the surface. If it is green, the fruit should be left on the tree; if it is pink, it may take further ripening. In a day or two it will be soft and ready to eat. Is the fruit as good as Latin Americans insist? Some hold that it tastes like a sweet pumpkin or a sweet potato but for the devotee no other fruit can compare with it.

MAMEY SAPOTE ICE CREAM

½ cup sugar	1 cup pureed mamey sapote
½ cup corn syrup	Juice of 1 lemon
Sprinkle of salt	2 eggs
1 cup milk	1 cup whipping cream

Mix the sugar, corn syrup, salt and the milk. Add the mamey sapote and lemon juice. Mix well. Beat the eggs and add to the fruit mixture. Be sure this is mixed well. Whip the cream and fold into the fruit mixture. Pour into refrigerator trays and freeze. Stir several times during the freezing process.

MAMEY SAPOTE MILK SHAKE

Place peeled, pitted and cut up mamey fruit in a blender with an equal amount of milk and sweetening to taste. Blend and serve in tall glasses with ice cubes.

MAMEY SAPOTE PINEAPPLE SHERBET

1½ cups sugar	1 cup pineapple juice
1 tsp. gelatin	Juice of 1 lemon
1½ cups pureed mamey sapote	2 eggs, separated

Dissolve sugar in ¾ cup water. Soak gelatin in ¼ cup cold water. Dissolve the gelatin in the sugar water. Add mamey sapote, lemon juice, and pineapple juice. Pour into a refrigerator tray and freeze to mush. Put into a mixing bowl and beat well. Add stiffly beaten egg whites. Return to tray and freeze.

Mango

Universally considered one of the finest of fruits, the mango is probably a more important fruit in the tropics than is the apple in the temperate zones. Cultivated in India for more than 4,000 years, it reached Florida in the early 1800s. Fruit is variable in size, shape, color, and flavor. Color is greenish, yellow, or red, and size varies from a few ounces to over 5 pounds. Smooth and leathery skin covers thick, luscious, yellow flesh enclosing a large, woody, husked seed. Mature fruit will ripen on the tree, but when some fruits change from green to yellow, the fruit can be picked and will ripen in about a week if kept at 70° to 75°. Storage at 55° will delay ripening. Fruit is best eaten out of hand off the tree but has a myriad of other uses.

FRESH MANGO ICE CREAM

Ripe mangos
2 cups sugar
Juice ½ lime
5 eggs

3 cups milk
Salt
1½ pt. whipping cream

Put the sugar in a quart refrigerator container. Puree enough mangos to fill the quart container. Add lime juice and mix well. Put in refrigerator and chill.

Make a boiled custard by mixing the eggs, milk, and salt thoroughly. Put in double boiler and cook until custard coats spoon. Remove from fire immediately, cool. Put in refrigerator for an hour or more.

When ready to make ice cream, put whipping cream in large mixing bowl. Whip at high speed for one to two minutes — do not overbeat! Add the custard and the pureed mangos. Mix well with a large spoon or spatula. Freeze. This recipe makes one gallon.

FROZEN MANGOS

Freezing the whole mango is not advised. Varieties with very little fiber should be chosen. Select fruit at the peak of ripeness, peel, and cut into ¼-inch slices or cubes. Place fruit individually on a cookie sheet and freeze as quickly as possible. Remove from freezer and quickly pack in freezer bags or cartons, seal, and return to freezer. Frozen slices are best served while a few ice crystals are still in the fruit.

FROZEN MANGO PUREE

Mangos can be frozen as puree and later used for cooking and in ice creams or punches. Peel the fruit and slice flesh into a blender. Press the puree through several thicknesses of cheese cloth to remove fiber. Pour into freezer cartons, leaving an inch of head space for expansion. Seal and freeze. Frozen mangos will still have good flavor after a year.

INDIAN CHUTNEY

6 lb. sliced ripe mangos	3 tsp. ground allspice
1½ lb. brown sugar	½ oz. salt
1 pt. vinegar	I lb. seedless raisins
I lb. preserved ginger or	2 oz. chopped onion
1 Tbsp. ground ginger	2 oz. chopped garlic
4 small hot pepper, chopped	2 tsp. mustard seed
3 tsp. ground cloves	½ lb. nuts, preferably almonds
	3 tsp. nutmeg

Mix all the ingredients. Bring to a boil and let stand overnight. Cook several hours or until dark and well blended. Seal hot in sterilized jars.

MANGO BUTTER

1 pt. peeled mangos	2½ cups sugar
(not quite ripe)	¼ cup lemon juice
¼ cup chopped ginger root	1 pkg. pectin

Grind the mangos through a coarse food chopper. Put into a saucepan, cover with water, and add ginger in a small cheesecloth bag. Place on low heat and simmer until tender. Remove from heat and press through a sieve or food mill, saving the juice. Discard the ginger. Add sugar and ·return to heat. Cook slowly until reduced to a thick consistency. Remove from heat and add pectin. Stir until cooled slightly and pour into hot sterilized jars.

MANGO CHUTNEY

7 lb. green and hard, and ripe
mangos (half of each)
peeled and diced
6 large onions, chopped
2 cloves garlic, chopped fine
6 oz. preserved ginger,
chopped fine or
3 Tbsp. fresh ginger root
1¼ quarts cider vinegar
1 cup lime juice
2 lb. light brown sugar
4 Tbsp. salt

1 cup tamarind pulp (optional)
3 chili peppers, chopped fine
(or about 1 Tbsp. chili powder)
1 tsp. crushed pepper
1 Tbsp. whole mustard seeds
1 Tbsp. celery seed
1 Tbsp. cinnamon
1½ tsp. whole cloves
1 Tbsp. allspice
1 box each raisins and currents
or white and cark raisins
1 cup nuts

In large kettle with cover, mix together vinegar, sugar, salt, chili peppers, and pepper. Bring mixture to boil, stirring often. Add all other ingredients, mixing well. Remove from heat, cover, and let stand overnight. Mix thoroughly next day and simmer gently 4 or 5 hours or until mango pieces have all turned color and are just tender. Do not overcook. Stir often to avoid sticking. Place in hot, sterilized jars and seal.

MANGO CRISP

1 cup siften flour
1 cup sugar
1 tsp. baking powder
¾ tsp. salt
1 tsp. cinnamon

1 tsp. nutmeg
1 egg
⅓ cup melted shortening
½ cup chopped pecans
4 cups mango, peeled and sliced

Line buttered 8 x 8 x 2" baking dish with mango slices. Sift dry ingredients together and work in egg with pastry blender until consistency of coarse meal. Sprinkle over mango slices. Drizzle the melted butter over the top, followed by the chopped nuts. Bake at 375° for 45 minutes.

MANGO CUSTARD PIE

Line a 9-inch pie plate with pastry and bake at 400° for five minutes. Remove from oven and fill with the following prepared custard mixture.

2 cups mango puree
¼ cup sifted flour
¾ cup sugar
½ tsp. cinnamon

1 Tbsp. lime juice
¼ cup evaporated milk
2 eggs beaten separately
added last

Return to the oven (350°) and bake for 30 minutes or more.

MANGO DAIQUIRI

⅓ cup of fully ripe mango
⅓ cup lime juice
3 Tbsp. sugar

⅓ cup rum
4 cups crushed ice

Combine all ingredients in a blender and blend until smooth.

MANGO MINCEMEAT

2 lb. beef (lean)
Water to cover
1 lb. suet
4 lb. mangos
4 cups sugar
2 lb. currants
3 lb. seedless raisins
½ lb. citron, cut fine

Juice and grated rind of
 2 oranges
Juice and grated rind of
 2 lemons
1 pt. fruit juice or cider
1 Tbsp. salt
1¼ tsp. grated nutmeg
½ tsp. mace

Cook beef slowly in water to cover until quite tender, about 3 hours. Cool and force through food chopper with suet and mangos, using coarse blade. Add remaining ingredients; mix thoroughly. Cook slowly 1 hour. Seal in sterilized jars. Makes 10 to 12 pints.

MANGO NUT BREAD

½ cup butter or
 vegetable shortening
¾ cup sugar
2 eggs
⅔ cup mango puree

2 cups sifted flour
1 tsp. soda
1 Tbsp. lime juice
¼ tsp. salt
½ cup chopped nuts

Cream shortening and sugar. Add eggs. Stir in dry ingredients. Mix mango and lime juice. Mix all ingredients together. Bake in a loaf pan at 350° for 1 hour. Mango bread is better if it is cut two or three days after baking.

MANGO PICCALILLI

1 qt. mango, peeled and chopped
2 large onions, chopped
6 green peppers, chopped
2 large hot peppers, chopped
1 Tbsp. salt

1 Tbsp. mustard seed
1 Tbsp. celery seed
4 cups sugar
1 cup vinegar
2 cups raisins

Combine all ingredients and bring to a boil, simmer for 10 minutes. Cover and let stand overnight; then cook until slightly thickened stirring all the time (about 45 minutes). Sterilize 4-pint jars; pour in hot mixture and seal.

MANGO PIE

Make a rich pie crust. Peel ripe (or a little underripe) mangos. Slice very thin. Line pie plate with crust, add one layer of sliced mangos; sprinkle with sugar, lemon, or lime juice and a very little cinnamon or nutmeg. Add rest of sliced mangos; top with sugar, spice, and lemon or lime juice and bits of butter. Cover or crisscross with pie crust. Bake about 40 minutes at 375°.

MANGO-GINGER PRESERVES

2 qts. ripe mango pieces	1 oz. fresh ginger root
½ cup lime juice	(peeled and cut in thin slices)
5 cups sugar	

Prepare mangos. Put all ingredients in heavy-weight pan. Place on heat. Stir until sugar is dissolved. Allow to cook rapidly, stirring occasionally until thickened. Fill sterilized jars with the preserves and seal. To insure good keeping, place in a pan of hot water deep enough to cover tops of jars. Allow to boil 5 minutes. Remove from bath. Cool and store.

MANGO-PINEAPPLE PRESERVES

2 qts. ripe mango pieces	¼ cup lime juice
1 No. 2 can crushed pineapple	4 cups sugar

Prepare mangos. Put all ingredients in heavy-weight pan. Place on heat. Stir until sugar is dissolved. Allow to cook rapidly, stirring occasionally until the preserves are thickened. Fill jars with the preserves and seal. To insure good keeping, place in a pan of hot water deep enough to cover tops of jars. Allow to boil 5 minutes. Remove from bath. Cool and store.

MANGO SHERBET

2 cups thick unsweetened green mango sauce	2 cups sugar
⅓ to ½ cup lime juice	¼ cup water
3 cups milk	1 egg white

Make the mango sauce as you would make unsweetened apple sauce. Dissolve sugar in water by bringing to the boiling point, cool, and add to milk, fruit, and lime juice. Add slightly beaten egg white, pour into freezing container and freeze. The mixture may curdle but this does not affect the finished product.

MANGO SMOOTHEE

1 cup milk	1 Tbsp. lime juice
1 cup mango puree,	1 cup finely crushed ice
sweetened to taste	Dash of salt

Have all ingredients chilled. Combine all ingredients in a jar with a tight sealing cover. Shake vigorously until ice is almost all dissolved. Serve immediately with ginger wafers or cookies.

MANGO SUPREME

4 cups mango pulp	1 cup milk
3 eggs, separated	1 cup cream, whipped
½ cup sugar	Salt

Cream egg yolks and sugar until mixture is light and fluffy. Add a pinch of salt to egg whites and beat until they are stiff. Fold egg whites into sugar mixture. Add whipped cream and milk. Mix well. Pour into refrigerator tray to freeze for 15 minutes. Stir well. Freeze 15 minutes more. Remove to large chilled bowl. Add chilled mango pulp and blend well. Return to freezer tray for 1 hour.

MANGO UPSIDE DOWN CAKE

2 cups sliced ripe mangos	1 egg
2 Tbsp. lemon juice	½ cup milk
1 Tbsp. margarine	1¼ cups flour
⅓ cup brown sugar	2 tsp. baking powder
¼ cup margarine	¼ tsp. salt
¾ cup sugar	

Pour lemon juice over mangos and let stand 15 minutes. Melt 1 Tbsp. margarine in 8 inch cake pan or casserole. (Do not use iron skillet as mangos will darken.) Add brown sugar and cover with mango slices.

To prepare cake batter, cream margarine; add sugar and cream; add beaten egg. Sift dry ingredients and add alternately with milk. Pour over mangos and bake 50 to 60 minutes at 375°. When cake is done, turn upside down and serve while warm.

QUICK MANGO JAM

4 cups pureed mango	7½ cups sugar
2 Tbsp. lime juice	1 bottle liquid pectin

Combine first 3 ingredients, mix well, and bring to a full rolling boil. Boil hard for 1 minute, stirring constantly. Remove from heat and at once stir in liquid pectin. Ladle into sterilized glasses and seal. Makes about 12 six-ounce glasses.

QUICK MANGO NUT BREAD

1 cup sugar
¼ cup cooking oil
2 eggs, beaten
1 cup pureed mangos

2 cups quick bread mix
½ cup grated coconut
  or chopped nuts

Heat oven to 350°. Cream sugar and shortening. Add eggs, mangos, and baking mix. Mix well. Add nuts or coconut. Mix. Pour in a well greased loaf pan with bottom lined with wax paper. Bake 50 minutes. Cool on rack 30 minutes before removing from pan.

SPICED MANGOS

4 lbs. ripe mangos, peeled
  and cut into pieces
2 lbs. sugar
1 cup vinegar

½ cup water
1 Tbsp. whole cloves
1 stick cinnamon

Prepare fruit. Then make a syrup of vinegar, water, and sugar with spices tied loosely in cheesecloth bag. Add the prepared fruit and boil until the fruit begins to look clear. Allow to stand until the next morning. Heat to boiling point and seal in sterilized jars.

SUNDAE MANGO SUPREME

Vanilla ice cream
Fresh mangos, sliced

Sweet orange wine
  (Cointreau, or Curacao)

Serve scoops of ice cream in sherbet glasses. Top with slices of mango and dribble the orange wine (or liqueur) over the mango slices.

SUPREME FRUIT SALAD

1 cup ripe mangos
1 large or 2 small bananas
1 cup pineapple

1 cup avocado
1 cup seeded grapes
½ cup grated coconut

Fruit should be ripe but firm. Make a dressing using ½ cup mayonnaise, 1 tablespoon sugar, 1/8 teaspoon salt, and 1 tablespoon lime juice. Put dressing and fruit in refrigerator for 1 hour. Immediately before serving cut fruit into ¾ inch pieces. Stir dressing well and mix with fruit. Serve on crisp lettuce leaf. Sprinkle with fresh grated coconut.

Monstera

The bold, cut-work leaves of this creeping or climbing plant are monstrous. The cone-like, "roasting ear" fruits, tasting like a mixture of pineapple and banana, are delicious; hence, the name. When the fruit is mature, the segmented covering of the edible portion begins to separate, starting at the stem end. Pick the fruit and put it in a closed plastic bag for several days. The fruit will ripen so that the entire fruit can be used; otherwise, only an inch or so ripens every day. Unless used promptly after ripening, the fruit will darken. Remove the fruit segments from the core and eat either plain or with sugar and cream, or use in the following recipes.

MONSTERA COCKTAIL

Remove fruit segments and combine as desired with chopped celery, onion, avocado with sauce of catsup, lime juice, salt and pepper.

MONSTERA FRUIT CUP

Place ripened sections in a large bowl with one quart of cold water and one cup of sweetened condensed milk. Mix and chill in refrigerator for one hour. If too sweet, add lime juice.

MONSTERA PRESERVE

Prepare 2 cups of fruit segments. Put fruit in colander and rinse with boiling water. Add ½ cup of water and simmer in a covered kettle for 10 minutes. Add 1 cup of sugar and 1 tablespoon of lime juice, and cook for an additional 20 minutes. Pour into sterilized jars and seal.

MONSTERA SALADS

1. Combine Monstera segments with sliced olives and a little lime juice. Serve in the halved avocado. Add French or mayonnaise dressing.
2. Combine Monstera segments with chopped nuts and apples, dressed with mayonnaise.
3. Combine Monstera segments with orange sections, sliced strawberries, or Surinam cherries. Serve with sliced guavas and mayonnaise.
4. Add Monstera segments to diced, cooked chicken and diced celery. Serve on lettuce with mayonnaise.
5. Add 1 cup of mashed Monstera pulp to lime gelatine, either alone or with chopped vegetables for a molded salad.

Mysore Raspberry

The Mysore raspberry is a tropical black raspberry quite like that of the temperate zone. This thorny, vinelike, shrub produces large quantities of juicy, slightly sweet fruits with a mild raspberry flavor. Flowers appear in the spring and fruit, by April-May. A well fertilized, well watered large bush will provide a pint of ripe berries every other day for 2-4 weeks. The berries are tasty with cream, with breakfast cereal, on vanilla ice cream, in pies and tarts, and they also make good jam.

MARYLAND RASPBERRY SHRUB

1 qt. raspberry juice
½ lb. sugar

1 pt. Jamaica rum or
half brandy

Mix well and bottle.

RASPBERRY AND APPLE JAM

3 cups sour apples, pared,
  cored and chopped
3 cups raspberries

4 cups sugar
1 cup water

Boil sugar and water until it spins a thread. Add apples. Boil 2 minutes and then add raspberries and boil another 10 minutes. Immediately pour into hot, sterilized, self-sealing jars and seal.

RASPBERRY COBBLER

For Shortcake Topping

1 cup flour
1 Tbsp. sugar
1½ tsp. baking powder
½ tsp. salt
3 Tbsp. shortening
½ cup milk

3 cups raspberries
1 cup sugar
1 Tbsp. cornstarch
1 cup boiling water
½ Tbsp. butter
½ tsp. cinnamon

Prepare shortcake by sifting dry ingredients together, cut in shortening, and stir in milk to make a soft dough. Then, mix in a saucepan sugar, cornstarch, and boiling water. Boil one minute to thicken while stirring. Pour prepared fruit into a 10 x 6 x 2 inch pan. Add thickened sugar mix and drop the dough by the spoonfuls to cover fruit. Dot with butter and sprinkle with cinnamon. Bake in a 400° oven for 30 minutes.

RASPBERRY DEEP DISH PIE

Line sides of deep 1½ quart casserole with pastry made as follows:

3 cups all purpose flour	2 Tbsp. sugar
½ cup shortening	3 tsp. baking powder
½ tsp. salt	¾ cup milk

Blend the dry ingredients. Then add milk and stir to a stiff dough. Roll out ¼ inch thick.

Place 4 cups washed berries in dish. Cover with 1½ cups sugar and dot with 4 tablespoons butter. Cover with pastry and gash top. Sprinkle with sugar. Bake at 375° for 45 minutes. Serve hot with cream.

RASPBERRY-FILLED MERINGUES

4 egg whites	2 to 3 cups fresh raspberries
½ tsp. cream of tartar	1 cup heavy cream
1 cup granulated sugar	¼ to ½ cup sour cream
1 tsp. vanilla extract	

Combine the egg whites with cream of tartar and beat until frothy. Gradually add the sugar, one tablespoon at a time, and lastly add the vanilla. The whites should be very stiff and high.

Grease and flour a baking sheet. Make four individual meringues about three inches wide and one-half inch thick. Bake in a preheated 250° oven for one hour. Turn off the heat and allow to dry in the oven for two to four hours. Cool.

Whip the cream just to the point where it is about to thicken. Add the sour cream to taste. Fill the meringues with fresh whole raspberries and top with the cream.

RASPBERRY JUICE

Ripe berries may be mashed through a fine sieve and the resulting pulpy juice used in punches without further processing. For juice to be preserved, the fruit should be cooked about 20 minutes with half as much water as fruit. Drain through a jelly bag.

RASPBERRY SYRUP

Mash equal quantities of raspberries and sugar; let stand overnight. Add one eighth as much water as berries and cook for 20 minutes. Strain through jelly bag. Again bring to a boil and pour into self-sealing sterilized glass jars. Use in beverages, ices, and sauces.

Papaya

This large, yellow- or orange-skinned fruit resembles a melon in many ways. An individual fruit may be as large as a soccer ball and weigh 10 to 15 pounds. Best eaten like melon enhanced with lime juice, papaya may also be used in drinks, preserves, fruit salads, and cooked desserts.

BAKED PAPAYA WITH MEAT FILLING

5 to 6 pound papaya cut
lengthwise into halves and
seeded
3 Tbsp. vegetable oil
½ cup finely chopped onions
½ tsp. finely chopped garlic
1 lb. lean ground beef

4 medium tomatoes, peeled,
and finely chopped (or 1½ cups
chopped canned tomatoes
1 tsp. chopped fresh chilies
1 tsp. salt
Freshly ground black pepper
4 Tbsp. Parmesan cheese

Preheat the oven to 350°. In a heavy 10-12 inch skillet, heat the oil moderately and drop in the onions and garlic. Stirring frequently, cook for about 5 minutes. Stir in the beef and cook until all traces of pink disappear. Add the tomatoes, chilies, salt, and a few grindings of pepper.

Spoon the meat mixture into the papaya shells. Place the shells in a shallow roasting pan and pour in enough boiling water to come about 1 inch up the sides of the papayas. Bake for 1 hour. Then sprinkle each shell with 1 tablespoon of the cheese and bake 30 minutes.

To serve, sprinkle papaya shells with remaining cheese.

GINGERED PAPAYA POSSUM

½ cup tepid water
2 pkg. dry yeast
2¼ cups all purpose flour
¾ cup sugar
1 tsp. salt
½ cup shortening
2 eggs, beaten

1 cup cooked papaya pulp
1 cup chopped dates
1 cup chopped black walnuts
1 Tbsp. grated fresh ginger root
or 1 tsp. powdered ginger
2 Tbsp. wheat germ
2 Tbsp. soy flour

Dissolve yeast in tepid water and let rise. Mix flour, sugar and salt; cut in butter and add eggs. Blend together papaya, dates, black walnuts, ginger, wheat germ, and soy flour. Using dough hook or mixer combine all ingredients, mix well, and let rise one hour. Stir down. Fill greased loaf pans half full and let rise. Set a shallow pan of water in bottom of oven. Heat oven to 375° and when dough has risen, bake 35-40 minutes. Turn pans on side to cool. Serve cold slices with cream cheese.

GOLDEN PAPAYA SALAD

2 cups pineapple juice
1 pkg. lemon or orange gelatin
1 cup papaya cubes

1 cup orange sections
¼ cup Surinam cherries, seeded,
or ½ cup sliced kumquats

Heat half of pineapple juice to boiling point. Dissolve gelatin in it and add remaining juice. Chill. When gelatin congeals, add fruit. Turn into molds and chill. Serve on lettuce with mayonnaise and Surinam cherries.

PALM BEACH GOLD

½ cup confectioner's sugar
8 marshmallows
1 cup shredded pineapple
1½ cups papaya in round balls

1 cup orange segments
1 cup whipped cream
2 tsp. lemon or lime juice

Whip cream, add sugar, then marshmallows cut in fourths. Fold in papaya, orange, and pineapple. Chill well before serving.

PAPAYA CATSUP

14 cups strained papaya pulp
4 Tbsp. whole allspice
3 Tbsp. whole cloves
3 Tbsp. mustard seed
1 stick cinnamon
1 piece ginger root, chopped

1 large onion, sliced
⅛ tsp. red pepper
6 Tbsp. sugar
2 Tbsp. salt
1⅓ cups vinegar
¼ tsp. tartaric acid

Tie spices and onion in a cheesecloth bag, add to papaya, and cook slowly for 40 minutes. Add sugar, salt, vinegar, and tartaric acid. Cook until thick. Remove spices. Pour into sterilized jars and seal.

PAPAYA CHUTNEY

6 cups peeled papaya,
cut up small
1 pt. vinegar
1 lb. raisins
¼ lb. blanched almonds
½ Tbsp. white mustard seed

½ cup chopped onions
1 tsp. hot peppers
3 Tbsp. ginger root
¾ lb. brown sugar
1 Tbsp. salt
½ cup chopped sweet pepper

To vinegar add sugar and bring to boil. Add all other ingredients and boil about 30 minutes. Pack in hot sterilized jars.

PAPAYA COCONUT PIE

1 cup sugar
½ tsp. salt
½ tsp. cinnamon
¼ tsp. cloves
2 beaten eggs
1 cup rich milk

1½ cups stewed papaya
½ cup grated coconut
Unbaked pastry shell
Topping:
½ cup finely grated coconut
2 Tbsp. honey

Put papaya in blender and puree. Mix first 8 ingredients in order given. Fill unbaked pastry shell and bake 45 minutes, first with high heat and then moderate. When nearly cooked, top with remaining coconut, drizzle on warm honey, and return to oven to brown.

PAPAYA DELIGHT

1 cup whipping cream
¼ cup powdered sugar
8 large or 32 miniature
  marshmallows

½ cup shredded coconut
1½ cups ripe papaya cubes
½ cup diced orange
2 tsp. lemon juice

Chill cream and whip. Add sugar, marshmallows. Fold in papaya, lemon juice, orange, and coconut. Chill before serving.

PAPAYA ICE CREAM

1 cup sugar
2 cups milk
2 eggs, beaten
1 pt. cream, whipped

1½ cups ripe sieved papaya
½ tsp. cinnamon
½ tsp. nutmeg
¼ tsp. salt

Prepare and cook custard using the first three ingredients. Add the papaya and spices. Fold in the whipped cream and freeze.

PAPAYA JAM

6 cups ripe papaya pulp
5 cups sugar

½ cup lemon, lime or
  calamondin juice

Press ripe papaya through a coarse sieve, then measure. Boil briskly in a smooth, heavy aluminum saucepan or pressure boiler until thick enough for jam. Add lemon juice and sugar and continue boiling until thick and clear. Stir frequently in order to prevent scorching. When the desired consistency is obtained, pour into hot, clean jars and seal.

PAPAYA MILK SHERBET

1½ cups ripe papaya pulp
3 Tbsp. lemon or lime juice
½ cup orange juice

1½ cups milk
1 cup sugar

Press papaya pulp through a coarse sieve and combine with fruit juice. Dissolve sugar in milk, add fruit mixture gradually to milk, and freeze in an ice cream freezer.

PAPAYA ONO-ONO

4 cups ripe papaya pulp
1 cup passion fruit juice
  or nectar
½ cup lemon or lime juice
1½ cups guava juice or nectar

½ cup orange juice
4 cups unsweetened pineapple
  juice
1 cup sugar
½ cup water

Blend papaya, fruit juices, sugar, and water for two minutes. Chill, pour over cracked ice, and serve plain or garnished with sprig of fresh mint.

PAPAYA PICKLE

1 large green papaya, cut
  into small pieces
1 Tbsp. mixed pickle spice
1 cup sugar
½ cup cider vinegar

½ cup water
1 tsp. salt
1 stick cinnamon
1 small dried chili pepper
1 large clove garlic, crushed

Tie spices in bag. Bring to boil sugar, vinegar, cinnamon stick, pepper, garlic, and spice bag. Boil 5 minutes and add papaya pieces. Simmer 15 minutes or until papaya is transparent. Remove spice bag and place pickled bits into sterilized jars. Usually makes 2 cups.

PAPAYA PINEAPPLE MARMALADE

10 cups sliced firm ripe papayas
1 cup fresh shredded pineapple
½ cup orange juice
½ cup lemon juice

Grated rind of 1 orange and
  2 lemons
3 Tbsp. grated green ginger root
8 cups sugar

Combine all ingredients except sugar and boil for about 30 minutes or until somewhat thick. Add sugar, and cook together until clear and of consistency desired. Stir frequently to prevent burning and when as thick as desired, pour into hot, sterilized jars and seal immediately.

PAPAYA SAUCE CAKE

¼ cup butter
1 cup sugar
1 egg
1½ tsp. baking powder
½ tsp. salt
⅓ tsp. ground cinnamon
⅓ tsp. grated nutmeg

¼ tsp. ground ginger
1½ cups flour
2 tsp. lemon juice
½ cup seedless raisins, if desired
3 Tbsp. water
1 cup diced ripe papaya

Stew the papaya and water together until a soft, thick, smooth sauce is obtained. Cream butter, add sugar, mix well, and add beaten egg. Sift salt, baking powder, spices, and flour together. Add cooled papaya sauce and dry ingredients alternately to egg mixture. Fold in lemon juice and raisins, then pour into an oiled loaf-cake pan and bake in a moderate oven (350°) for 50 to 60 minutes.

PAPAYA SEED DRESSING

½ cup sugar
1 tsp. seasoned salt
1 tsp. dry mustard
1 cup white or tarragon vinegar

2 cups oil
1 small onion, minced
2 Tbsp. fresh papaya seeds

Place vinegar and dry ingredients in blender, turn on, and gradually add oil and onion. Add seeds and blend only until the seeds are the size of coarse ground pepper. Good with fruit or green salads.

PAPAYA UPSIDE-DOWN CAKE

2 cups Jiffy Baking Mix
⅔ cup milk
1 cup sugar
1 cup mashed papaya

½ cup brown sugar
⅓ cup butter or margarine
Nuts and cherries
for garnish

Slice enough papaya (½ inch thick) to cover bottom of pans. Mix first four ingredients, mix well, and put aside. In 8 or 9 inch cake pan, rub sides with butter and melt rest in bottom of pan. Sprinkle brown sugar on bottom of pan, add to this the papaya, nuts, and batter. Bake at 350° for 30 minutes or more. Garnish with cherries.

POLYNESIAN BAKED CHICKEN

2 cut up frying chickens	2 Tbsp. lime juice
1 cup flour	½ cup brown sugar
1 tsp. seasoned salt	1 Tbsp. cornstarch
½ lb. butter or margarine, melted	½ tsp. salt
1 cup orange juice	2 cups ripe papaya, sliced

Shake chicken in paper bag with flour and salt. Oil large baking dish with 2 Tbsp. of melted butter. Place chicken in baking dish and brush remaining butter over each piece. Bake 50 minutes at 350° or until chicken is browned. Meanwhile combine juices, sugar, salt and cornstarch in saucepan and bring to a boil, stirring constantly. When clear and thick, remove from heat and add papaya. Pour over chicken, coating each piece, and bake 10 minutes. Serve garnished with chopped parsley or green pepper and sesame seeds.

RIPE PAPAYA PIE

3 cups ripe papayas	4 Tbsp. tapioca
¾ cup sugar	4 Tbsp. butter
¼ cup calamondin, lemon, or lime juice	½ tsp. cinnamon
	Unbaked double pie shell

Slice papaya and add sugar, tapioca, and fruit juice. Let stand 10 minutes. Fill bottom pie shell with mixture. Add butter and cinnamon. Cover with top crust, which has been slit for several vents. Bake at 400° for 45 minutes until golden brown.

ROYAL HAWAIIAN DELIGHT

1 cup whipping cream	1½ cups ripe papaya cubes
¼ cup powdered sugar	½ cup diced orange
8 marshmallows	2 tsp. lemon juice
4 cups shredded doconut	1 tsp. salt

Chill cream and whip. Add sugar, then marshmallows cut into quarters. Fold in papaya, lemon juice, orange, and coconut. Pour into serving dish or individual glass dishes. Chill before serving.

Passion Fruit

Many species of the Passiflora genus produce edible fruit. The small fruit species have round to oval, brittle-shelled, 2-inch fruits that contain many seeds imbedded in a gelatinous, aromatic juicy pulp, which is eaten from the shell with a spoon or used in drinks. Another group includes the giant granadilla, which reaches 12 inches in length and weighs to 6 pounds. Both the pulp and thick flesh are edible. The thick flesh may be eaten like a melon or mixed in fruit salads. The green fruit may be boiled and used as a vegetable. If served chilled and sliced as a dessert, the flesh of the giant granadilla is improved when sprinkled with a bit of powdered coriander or lime juice.

FRESH PASSION FRUIT PUNCH

1⅓ cups fresh passion
    fruit juice
1⅓ cups pineapple juice
1⅓ cups water

2 cups sugar
2 Tbsp. lemon juice
1 qt. ginger ale
1⅓ cups pureed soursop

Press passion fruit pulp through a coarse sieve or food mill to obtain juice. Add remaining ingredients and chill. Serve over cracked ice.

HOT SPICED PASSION FRUIT JUICE

3¾ cups water
⅞ cup sugar
Lemon slices
18 whole cloves
18 whole allspice

3 pieces stick cinnamon
    (2 inches long)
¾ cup passion fruit juice
1 Tbsp. lemon juice

Combine all ingredients except fruit juices. Boil 10 minutes in a covered container, stirring occasionally. Add passion fruit and lemon juice and heat to the simmering point. Strain and serve hot with lemon slices.

PASSION FRUIT CAKE ICING

3 Tbsp. butter
2¼ cups confectioner's sugar

¼ cup fresh passion fruit pulp
    or 3 Tbsp. passion fruit syrup

Press passion fruit pulp through a sieve to remove seeds. Cream butter adding 1/3 cup of sugar gradually. Add fruit pulp and remaining sugar. Beat until the mixture is smooth and stiff enough to spread on cake.

PASSION FRUIT COCONUT CANDY

½ cup passion fruit pulp
2½ cups dry shredded coconut

5 cups confectioner's sugar
English walnuts

Press fruit pulp through sieve to remove seeds. Add two-thirds of the sugar. Beat until creamy. Add one-half of the coconut and sugar to form soft balls. Roll balls in coconut and place on a buttered pan. Garnish with nuts. Harden candy at least 8 hours in a cold place.

PASSION FRUIT DELICIOUS

2 Tbsp. butter
¾ cup sugar
½ cup flour
1 tsp. baking powder

2 eggs, separated
1¼ cup milk
2 Tbsp. passion fruit juice

Cream butter and sugar, add egg yolks, flour, milk and passion fruit juice. Fold in stiffly beaten egg whites, pour into greased 9" pie tin, stand in a pan of hot water, and bake at 425° for 10 minutes. Reduce heat to 350° and bake until set . Serve cold with custard sauce.

PASSION FRUIT GELATIN

½ cup passion fruit juice
1 cup hot water

½ cup sugar
1 Tbsp. unflavored gelatin

Soak gelatin in ½ cup cold water. Mix gelatin, hot water, and sugar. Stir over low heat until smooth. Cool. Add fruit juice and pour into mold. Chill.

PASSION FRUIT ICE CREAM

½ cup passion fruit juice
2 cups thin cream

½ cup sugar
½ Tbsp. vanilla

Mix all ingredients and stir until sugar is dissolved. Freeze.

PASSION FRUIT JELLY

3 cups fresh passion fruit juice
1 cup water

7½ cups sugar
1 bottle liquid pectin

Measure sugar into saucepan; add juice and water. Bring to boil, stirring constantly. Add pectin. Bring to rolling boil for 1 minute — stirring constantly. Pour into sterilized glasses.

PASSION FRUIT MOUSSE

½ Tbsp. gelatin
2 Tbsp. cold water
3 Tbsp. boiling water

1¼ cups passion fruit syrup
1 cup whipping cream

Soak gelatin in cold water. Add boiling water and heat mixture until the gelatin is dissolved. Whip cream. Fold in syrup and gelatin. Freeze.

PASSION FRUIT SAUCE

½ cup sugar
1⅓ Tbsp. cornstarch
¼ tsp. salt
Dash ground ginger

½ cup boiling water
2 Tbsp. margarine
⅔ cup passion fruit juice

Mix together sugar, cornstarch, salt, and ginger. Add water gradually. Cook over medium heat until sauce is thickened, stirring constantly. Add margarine and fruit juice. Bring to boil. Remove from heat. Serve hot with hotcakes, baked bananas, or banana shortcake.

PASSION FRUIT SHERBET

¼ cup sugar
2 cups water

¼ cup fresh passion fruit juice
1 egg white

Combine sugar and water and heat to the boiling point. When the mixture is cool, add passion fruit and unbeaten egg white. Freeze.

PASSION FRUIT SYRUP

4 cups water
6 cups sugar

2⅔ cups passion fruit pulp or
2 cups passion fruit juice

Add sugar to water and heat to the boiling point. Add pulp and bring to boil. Pour into hot sterile bottles and seal at once. Syrup keeps well 6 to 8 months and may be used for drinks, cake icings, and frozen desserts.

PASSIONATE PIE

½ cup passion fruit juice
   (sieved)

1 can condensed milk
3 egg yolks

Beat all together until very thick and creamy. Pour into crumb crust. Top with whipped cream.

Persimmon

This large, bright yellow to orange, globose fruit is 1½ to 4 inches in diameter. Although unpleasantly astringent when hard and immature, fully ripe fruit is soft and sweet with jellylike flesh. Fruit should be picked when it begins to soften; by snipping off a bit of the stem with the fruit it will continue to ripen. Ripe fruit is delicious eaten fresh.

PERSIMMON CAKE I

3 cups flour	1 cup vegetable oil
2 cups sugar	3 eggs, slightly beaten
1 tsp. ground cinnamon	1½ cups persimmon pulp
½ tsp. salt	1 cup chopped walnuts
1 tsp. soda	Powdered sugar

Combine first 9 ingredients, mixing well. Pour into greased and floured Bundt pan. Bake at 325° for 1 hour. Remove from pan while warm. Dust with powdered sugar.

PERSIMMON CAKE II

2 cups sugar	2 tsp. cinnamon
3 Tbsp. butter or margarine	½ tsp. cloves
2 cups persimmon pulp	½ tsp. allspice
2 cups chopped walnuts	½ tsp. nutmeg
1 cup seedless raisins	4 tsp. soda
Grated rind, 1 orange	3 tsp. baking powder
1 cup milk	2 tsp. vanilla
4 cups sifted cake flour	

Cream sugar and butter. Add remaining ingredients, in order, and mix well. Bake in greased loaf tins or four small pans for 1½ hours at 300°.

PERSIMMON FRUIT PUREE DRESSING

1 cup cream cheese	1 tsp. honey
⅓ cup orange juice	Dash of salt
1 Tbsp. lemon juice	½ cup sieved persimmon pulp

Mash the cream cheese until soft. Cream in orange juice, lemon, honey and salt. Add persimmon pulp and beat. Serve on fruit salad.

PERSIMMON GELATIN

1 Tbsp. unflavored gelatin
¼ cup cold water
⅓ cup hot water

¾ cup persimmon pulp
1 tsp. lemon juice
2 egg whites

Dissolve gelatin in cold water. Add hot water, persimmon pulp, and lemon juice. Refrigerate until set. Fold in egg whites beaten until stiff. Pour into sherbet glasses and chill in refrigerator about 1 hour.

PERSIMMON MOUSSE

1½ cups ripe persimmon pulp
¼ cup diced orange
½ cup diced canned pineapple

¼ cup sugar
1 Tbsp. lemon juice
1 cup evaporated milk (whipped)

Combine persimmon pulp with remaining ingredients and fold in the whipped milk. Pour into a mold or refrigerator tray and freeze.

PERSIMMON PIE

1 8-inch baked pie shell
2 cups persimmon pulp
½ cup sugar
½ tsp. mace
1 tsp. lemon rind (grated)

2 tsp. butter
2 beaten egg yolks
2 stiffly beaten egg whites
4 Tbsp. sugar

Force persimmon pulp through a colander and add sugar which has been mixed with mace and lemon rind. Place over low heat. Add butter and beaten yolks. Cook and stir until mixture is slightly thickened. Pour into baked pie shell and cool. Cover with meringue made from whites and 4 Tbsp. sugar. Brown as desired in a moderate oven (350°).

PERSIMMON PUDDING

1 cup persimmon pulp
2 well beaten eggs
1 cup milk
1½ Tbsp. melted butter
1 cup sifted enriched flour
½ tsp. baking soda

¾ cup sugar
½ tsp. salt
¼ tsp. cinnamon
¼ tsp. nutmeg
½ cup raisins or chopped nuts

Mix and sift flour, soda, sugar, salt and spices. Combine with the mixed persimmon, eggs, milk, and butter. Stir to a soft batter. Add more milk if necessary. Add raisins or nuts. Pour into a buttered pan. Bake at 350° 30 to 45 minutes. Serve with hard sauce or whipped cream.

Pineapple

The fruit of this bromeliad develops from the inflorescence at the end of the stem and consists of many seedless fruits fused together. Sizes range upward to 10 pounds; shapes are oval to cylindrical; colors are whitish, yellowish to orange.

APRICOT PINEAPPLE JAM

1 lb. dried apricots	¾ cup sugar to each cup fruit
1 large fresh pineapple	16 maraschino cherries

Soak the apricots in water to cover until soft. Pare and core the fresh pineapple. Drain the apricots and put both fruits through a food chopper. Save all juice. In a large heavy preserving kettle combine fruit, juice, and sugar. Stir until all sugar is dissolved. Add chopped cherries and bring to a boil. Cook over low heat until fruit is clear and jam is thick. Stir occasionally. Pour into hot sterilized jars and seal.

BACON ROLLUPS

Wrap pineapple chunks with bacon; fasten with a toothpick and broil; serve crisp and hot as appetizers.

BRANDY-PINEAPPLE CUSTARD

1 cup pineapple juice	5 eggs well beaten
¾ cup sugar	¼ cup brandy

Combine juice and sugar, heat to boiling point, cool. Add eggs and brandy. Cook over hot water until mixture coats spoon. Serve cold.

CREAMY PINEAPPLE FROSTING

½ cup butter or margarine softened	3 cups sifted confectioners' sugar
½ cup shortening	½ cup crushed pineapple (do not drain)

Cream butter or margarine, shortening, and sugar until fluffy. Add crushed pineapple; stir to combine. Frost Pineapple Cake (see recipe, p. 138).

DIVINE PARFAIT

1 cup sugar	1 cup crushed pineapple, drained
¾ cup water	1 cup heavy cream, whipped
3 egg whites, stiffly beaten	1 tsp. vanilla

Combine sugar and water in small saucepan. Attach candy thermometer to side of pan and cook to 236°. Beat egg whites and cream in separate bowls until stiff. Pour hot syrup over egg whites slowly, beating until cool. Fold in vanilla, crushed pineapple, and whipped cream. Freeze.

LATTICE PINEAPPLE PIE

½ cup sugar	1 Tbsp. butter
2 Tbsp. cornstarch	1 Tbsp. lemon juice
¼ tsp. salt	Pastry for 2-crust 8 inch pie
2½ cups crushed pineapple	

Mix sugar, cornstarch, and salt. Add to pineapple in a saucepan. Heat stirring constantly until mixture boils; boil stirring about 2 minutes. Remove from heat and stir in butter and lemon juice. Pour into pastry lined pan. Weave pastry strips across top. Bake at 425° until browned.

LEBANESE PINEAPPLE

1 small pineapple	¼ cup fine granulated sugar
1 orange	3 egg whites
½ lb. seedless green grapes	¼ cup honey
Juice of ½ lemon	3 Tbsp. toasted shredded almonds
1½ Tbsp. chopped crystalized ginger or chopped citron	2 strawberries

Prepare pineapple as for Philippine Pineapple Malacanan (see recipe, p. 137). Save shells.

Combine the diced pineapple with: the orange, peeled, diced and stripped of all white membrane; the grapes, washed and stemmed; lemon juice; 1 Tbsp. of the ginger or citron (save ½ Tbsp. for the garnish). Blend this mixture and sweeten to taste. Spoon the mixture back into shells. Heap with meringue made as follows: Beat 3 egg whites until they stand in stiff peaks. Blend in the honey. Mound this mixture on top of the fruit-filled shells, making sure to spread the meringue to the side of the shells to keep it from shrinking. Sprinkle the meringue with almonds and remaining ginger or citron. Bake in hot oven, 400° for 5 minutes. Let the shells cool, then chill them. Serve each half shell with a strawberry perched on top.

PHILIPPINE PINEAPPLE MALACANAN

1 small pineapple
½ lb. seedless green grapes
1 fresh peach
Juice of ½ lemon
1 pint strawberries
2 Tbsp. Kirsch

¼ cup fine granulated sugar
2 bananas, chilled in skins
1 orange
½ cup chopped walnuts
2 large grape leaves or other
   leaves, for garnish

Cut the pineapple in halves. With a sharp knife cut the flesh from the shell. Remove the core. Cut into ¼-inch pieces.

Wash and stem grapes. Peel and thinly slice peach. Squeeze lemon juice over it to prevent darkening. Wash and stem strawberries, saving a few for the garnish. Combine the fruits, again squeezing a little lemon juice over all. Add the Kirsch and sweeten to taste. Spoon mixture into the shells and chill well before serving. Peel and slice the orange. Just before serving, peel the bananas, brush with lemon juice, and sprinkle with sugar. Then, slice the bananas and coat them with chopped nuts. Place the fruit-filled pineapple shells on a bed of grape leaves, surround them with the orange and banana slices, and add a scattering of strawberries.

PINEAPPLE AMBROSIA PIE

1¼ cups graham cracker crumbs
½ cup coconut
⅓ cup melted butter
1 pkg. (3 oz.) orange gelatin

1 cup boiling water
½ cup cold water
1 cup orange sherbet
1½ cups drained crushed pineapple

Combine graham cracker crumbs, coconut, and melted butter. Press into 10-inch pie plate. Bake at 350° for 10 minutes. Cool thoroughly.

Dissolve gelatin in boiling water. Add cold water, then orange sherbet. Stir until sherbet is melted. Add 1 cup of pineapple. Chill until thick and pineapple is suspended throughout. Pour into pie shell. Chill 3 hours. Garnish with reserved pineapple and whipped cream.

PINEAPPLE AND APPLE CONSERVE

1 qt. pineapple, diced or
   shredded
1 qt. diced tart apples

2 oranges, juice and grated rind
6 cups sugar
1½ cups shredded coconut

Cook the pineapple in ½ cup water until tender. Add the apple, orange juice and rind, and the sugar. Cook mixture until it is transparent. Add coconut and pack conserve into clean, hot jars. Seal at once.

PINEAPPLE BRAN MUFFINS

1 egg
2 Tbsp. melted shortening
¾ cup crushed pineapple
1¼ cups flour
6 Tbsp. sugar

1½ tsp. baking powder
¼ tsp. soda
¾ tsp. salt
½ cup bran flakes
⅓ cup chopped walnuts

Beat the egg; add the melted shortening and undrained pineapple. Sift together the flour, sugar, baking powder, soda, and salt; stir into the pineapple mixture. Add the bran flakes and nuts. Pour into well-oiled muffin pans and bake at 375° for 30 minutes.

PINEAPPLE, CABBAGE, MARSHMALLOW SALAD

½ medium-sized head cabbage
1 cup drained, crushed pineapple
½ cup cut marshmallows or
    miniature marshmallows

½ tsp. salt
1 Tbsp. sugar
½ cup sour cream, salad
    dressing, or mayonnaise

Chill cabbage thoroughly. Shred fine. Measure about 4 cups. Add marshmallows and drained crushed pineapple. Combine remaining ingredients; pour over cabbage mixture. Sprinkle with paprika.

PINEAPPLE CAKE

½ cup butter or margarine,
    softened
¾ cup sugar
3 egg yolks
2½ cups cake flour, sifted
2 tsp. baking powder
½ tsp. baking soda

½ tsp. salt
½ cup orange juice
1 tsp. vanilla
1 cup crushed pineapple
    (do not drain)
3 egg whites
¼ cup sugar

Cream butter or margarine and sugar until light and fluffy. Add egg yolks, one at a time, beating well after each addition. Sift dry ingredients together. Add to butter mixture alternately with orange juice, vanilla, and crushed pineapple, beginning and ending with flour.

Beat egg whites until foamy; gradually beat in ¼ cup sugar. Beat until stiff and glossy. Fold egg whites into batter gently but thoroughly. Pour batter into two greased and floured 8-inch cake pans. Bake at 350° 25-30 minutes. Frost with Creamy Pineapple Frosting (see recipe, p. 135).

PINEAPPLE CHICKEN

2 lb. chicken thighs	¾ cup unsweetened pineapple
⅓ cup flour	juice
½ tsp. salt	2 Tbsp. soy sauce
¼ tsp. pepper	2 Tbsp. brown sugar, packed
¼ cup salad oil	1 cup pineapple chunks, drained

Dredge chicken thighs in flour, salt and pepper. Heat oil and brown chicken. Drain excess oil. Combine pineapple juice, soy sauce, and brown sugar. Pour over chicken, cover and simmer for 45 minutes. Add pineapple chunks and cook until heated through. Serve hot.

PINEAPPLE DAIQUIRI

¼ cup crushed pineapple	¼ tsp. lemon juice
3 Tbsp. light rum	4 ice cubes

Combine all in blender and whip at high speed about 30 seconds.

PINEAPPLE MOUSSE

¾ cup evaporated milk,	6 Tbsp. sugar
1 cup crushed pineapple	1 Tbsp. lemon juice

Stir sugar into pineapple and refrigerate. Whip evaporated milk until stiff, add lemon juice. Fold pineapple mixture into whipped milk. Freeze.

PINEAPPLE PRESERVES

1 lb. pineapple cut in cubes	¼ cup water
¾ lb. sugar	

Cook all ingredients until clear. Pour into sterilized jars and seal.

PINEAPPLE SHERBET

½ Tbsp. (½ envelope) gelatin	1 cup (9 oz.) crushed pineapple
2 Tbsp. cold water	1 tsp. vanilla
2 cups buttermilk	1 egg white, beaten
1 cup sugar	

Soften gelatin in cold water; dissolve over hot water and add buttermilk, sugar, pineapple and vanilla. Pour mixture into freezer tray; freeze firm. Then beat until smooth. Add egg white. Refreeze until firm.

PINEAPPLE TERIYAKIS

1 lb. tender top round or sirloin of beef, cut ¾" thick
2½ cups (1 No. 2 can) pineapple chunks, drained
½ cup syrup drained from chunks
¼ cup soy sauce
1 clove garlic, chopped fine
1 tsp. chopped fresh ginger root, or ¾ tsp. ground ginger
1 small jar stuffed olives, drained
22 short wooden or metal skewers (about 4 inches long)

With a sharp knife, cut meat into bite-size pieces, about the same size as the pineapple chunks. Combine pineapple syrup, soy sauce, garlic, and ginger; pour over meat cubes and set aside at room temperature for at least 1 hour. Alternate cubes of meat and pineapple chunks on skewers; then finish off with a stuffed olive. Broil 3 inches from heat, turning once, for 10 to 12 minutes. Serve very hot. This recipe makes 20 to 22 servings, sufficient as an appetizer for 8 to 10 persons. Teriyakis are equally good to serve with rice and a salad for luncheon or supper. In that case, cut meat in larger pieces and use longer skewers. The amounts given will be adequate for 4 to 5 persons.

POLYNESIAN PINEAPPLE SHRIMP

2½ cups pineapple chunks with syrup
½ cup sweet pickle chips, cut in half
3 Tbsp. pickle syrup
¾ tsp. salt
1 Tbsp. cornstarch
1 lb. cooked shrimp

Put pineapple, pickled, pickle syrup, and salt in saucepan. Dissolve cornstarch in a little water and add to saucepan. Bring mixture to a boil, stirring, until clear and thickened. Add the cooked shrimp and heat through. Serve on rice.

SUNSET SALAD

1 pkg. lemon flavored gelatin
2 Tbsp. lemon juice (or vinegar)
1½ cups grated raw carrots
1¼ cups well drained canned, crushed pineapple

Prepare gelatin according to directions on package. Add the lemon juice or vinegar. Chill, and when partially set, add grated carrots and crushed pineapple. When partially set again, pour into a ring mold (8½" in diameter and 2½" deep) or 8 to 10 individual molds. Chill until firm. Unmold on large chop plate or individual salad plates. Garnish with crisp lettuce or watercress. Serve with appropriate dressing: mayonnaise or salad dressing thinned with a little cream.

Plantain

This cooking banana is a staple in the diet of many people in the tropics and is a versatile fruit. It is used mature but hard and green as well as soft and yellow, and also fully ripe, mostly dark brown. One of the best ways to prepare ripe fruit is to slit the skin and bake at 350° until soft; serve with butter and brown sugar. Green fruit is added to soups and stews by Latin Americans.

FRIED GREEN PLANTAINS

Slice the ends off of two green plantains. Cut each in half and let stand in hot water for 5 minutes. Peel and dry with paper towels. Cut into 1 inch thick slices and fry in moderately hot oil for 7 minutes. Put slices of plantains between layers of paper towels. Press with the ball of the hand. Put flattened pieces back in the hot oil and fry until light brown. Remove from oil, drain on paper towels, and sprinkle lightly with salt. Serve with fried pork, beef, or chicken.

GREEN PLANTAIN CHIPS

Peel green plantains. Cut diagonally into very thin slices. Let stand in ice water to cover for ½ hour. Drain, pat dry. Fry in deep hot fat (370°) until lightly browned and crisp. Drain on paper towels, sprinkle with salt. Serve as a garnish with fruit salad or as an appetizer.

PINYON

1 lb. seasoned ground beef (see recipe, p. 144)	1 pkg. frozen French style string beans
2 or 3 ripe plantains	3 eggs

Cut plantains in half and slice lengthwise. Fry in butter until light brown. Beat eggs and season with a bit of salt. Arrange ingredients in a buttered casserole with plantains on the bottom and on the top. Bake in a 350° oven until eggs are well set.

PLANTAINS AND BACON

Slice ripe plantain in ¼ inch slices. Fry bacon, remove from pan. Fry plantain in the fat. Drain slices and mix with crumbled bacon.

PLANTAIN CASSEROLE

2 ripe plantains, cut into small pieces	3 Tbsp. sugar
6 Tbsp. butter	1 tsp. cinnamon
2 cups grated muenster cheese	3 eggs separated
	2 Tbsp. dry bread crumbs

Fry plantain slices in 2 Tbsp. butter until golden brown. Drain on paper towels. Mix cheese, sugar, and cinnamon. Beat egg yolks until thick, fold into beaten egg whites. Butter 1 qt. baking dish. Sprinkle with crumbs. Pour in ¼ egg mixture, ⅓ plantains, ⅔ cup cheese, dot with butter. Repeat layers, end with eggs. Bake at 350°.

RIPE PLANTAINS IN SYRUP

Cut plantains in four sections. Brown lightly in butter. Place in a sauce pan and add 1¼ cups sugar and ¾ cup water for each large plantain. Add stick cinnamon. Boil at moderate heat until the liquid is thick and syrupy.

STUFFED RIPE PLANTAINS

Slice ripe plantains lengthwise and fry in oil until light brown. When cool, make rings by pinning the ends together with toothpicks. Place the rings on a cookie sheet. Fill with seasoned meat filling and cover tops with beaten egg. Lift with a spatula and turn topside down to fry in hot oil. When the egg is set and lightly browned, turn the rings over, cover with beaten egg and fry on the other side.

Seasoned Meat Filling

2 Tbsp. ham or pork shoulder	½ cup tomato sauce
½ green pepper	6 olives
1 medium size onion	1 Tbsp. capers
1 tomato	
1 clove garlic	
1 tsp. oregano	
1 lb. ground beef	

Chop the first six ingredients in a food grinder or blender. Add to the ground beef and simmer for a few minutes. Add all other ingredients and mix well. Cook at moderate temperature until meat is tender.

Roselle

The edible portion of roselle is the large, red, fleshy calyx that surrounds the seed pod. About 3 weeks after the flower appears the calyxes should be harvested as later they become fibrous. The seed pod is easily removed by cutting the stem at the base of the calyx and pushing the pod out. Roselle makes jelly and sauce similar in color, texture, and flavor to cranberry.

ORANGE-ROSELLE RELISH

3 heaping cups roselle calyxes   ½ cup sugar
1 orange   2 Tbsp. mild honey

Put roselle and orange, cut in quarters with seeds and center membrane removed, through food chopper. Add sugar and honey and mix well.

ROSELLE CONSERVE

2 cups roselle   1 cup seeded or seedless raisins
1 large orange   3 cups sugar
    1 cup broken pecan meats

Grate rind from orange. Remove flesh and put through food chopper. Add one cup of water, let stand several hours Simmer until tender. Discard roselle seed pods, grind, add 3 cups water, combine with orange, and cook ten minutes. Add raisins and sugar and cook until mixture thickens. Add nuts and cook five minutes. Pour into jars and seal.

ROSELLE GELATIN SALAD

1 qt. roselle (with seed   ⅓ cup cold water
    pods removed)   1 cup diced celery
2 cups boiling water   ⅓ cup chopped pecan meats
2 cups sugar   Mayonnaise or boiled dressing
2½ Tbsp. gelatin   Lettuce

Cook roselle in water until tender. Rub through a sieve, add sugar, and cook five minutes. Add gelatin which has been dissolved in the cold water for five minutes. Just before this begins to set, pour half of the mixture into a shallow dish. Allow to set. Keep the remaining mixture warm. Over the first half sprinkle the diced celery and nuts. Pour the remaining half over this and allow to set. Cut into slices and serve on lettuce with salad dressing and a few extra nuts.

ROSELLE JELLY

Roselle makes an attractive red jelly. To prepare fruit, cut base of each calyx with a sharp knife, separate from seed pod, and wash well. Two measures of water to three of calyxes are used for making the extraction. Boil gently for 15 minutes, cover, and allow to cool. Strain through jelly bag and then measure one cup of roselle juice for ½ to ¾ cups sugar to make jelly. Boil briskly to jelly point (222°). Do not overcook.

ROSELLE PUNCH

1 qt. roselle juice   ¼ cup orange juice
(See first step, Roselle Jelly   Juice of ½ lemon
recipe, above)   Pinch of salt
¾ cup sugar

Combine all ingredients and stir until sugar is dissolved. Pour over cracked ice just before serving.

ROSELLE SALAD

On a chilled plate, arrange crisp lettuce leaves. In the center put a large spoonful of stiff roselle sauce (see recipe below) and sprinkle with cream cheese that has been put through a sieve. Add chopped pecans as a top garnish and serve with French dressing made with lemon juice.

ROSELLE SAUCE

When roselle is to be served as a sauce, use three measures of calyxes and two of water. Cook until tender, sweeten to taste, and allow sauce to come again to the boiling point in order to be certain that all the sugar is dissolved. The sauce should be rubbed through a coarse sieve. This gives an excellent imitation of a strained cranberry sauce.

TROPICAL RELISH

4 cups roselle calyxes   1 cup shredded kumquat or
1 orange   ½ kumquat and ½ calamondin,
1½ cups sugar   shredded or ground
1 cup shredded pineapple

Put roselle and orange, seeds removed, and other citrus through food chopper. Add pineapple and blend all with sugar. Chill in refrigerator several hours before using. Keeps well.

Sapodilla

Fruits are usually 2 to 4 inches in diameter, thin skinned, grayish or rusty brown, and globose to ovoid. The scruffy skin encloses a yellowish-brown, translucent, melting fragrant, sweet flesh carrying 10 to 12, hard, black, separated seeds. Fruit should be picked when mature but still hard and store in a cool place until soft. Ripe fruit are quite good eaten out of hand.

"DILLY" RICE

3 cups cooked rice	2 Tbsp. crystallized ginger
2 sapodillas	1 Tbsp. water
3 Tbsp. crystallized lemon peel	

Cut sapodillas into ½ inch pieces. Cut ginger and lemon peel into bits. Combine all ingredients in saucepan and heat until steaming hot.

SAPODILLA CREAM SHERBET

1 cup sapodilla puree	½ pint light cream
1 cup sugar	Sprinkle of salt
2 cups milk	1 tsp. lemon juice

Mix sugar, sapodilla puree, and lemon juice. Gradually add mixture to cream and milk. Freeze.

SAPODILLA CUSTARD

1½ cups milk	3 Tbsp. brown sugar
1¼ cups sapodilla puree	⅛ tsp. salt
3 eggs, beaten slightly	

Scald milk, then combine all ingredients. Pour into buttered custard cups, set in a pan of hot water. Bake at 325° for 30 minutes. Top with a bit of fruit. Serve warm.

SAPODILLA ICE CREAM

1½ cup sapodilla puree	½ cup sugar
¾ cup milk	1 cup whipped cream

Mix sugar with the puree. Add milk. Fold in the cream and freeze.

Seagrape

The seagrape is an interesting native much used as an ornamental and also as a producer of fruit. In late summer long clusters of grapelike berries hang in abundance from the branches. From late August into October these fruits turn purple and take on a velvetlike appearance. The thin pulp surrounding a large stone has an acid, slightly salty flavor. The fruit has sufficient pectin to produce excellent jelly. Clusters of fruit do not ripen evenly, so ripe berries can either be tediously pulled or dislodged by a rather rough running of a hand over the cluster. A simpler method is to spread a sheet under the tree and shake the branches.

SEAGRAPE JELLY

4 cups prepared juice	5 cups sugar
5 Tbsp. lime juice	1 box powdered pectin

Prepare juice as described under Seagrape Juice below. Place 4 cups juice in 4-8 quart pan and boil 3-4 minutes. Add the lime juice and a box of powdered pectin; stir and bring to a hard boil. Add sugar. Boil, stirring constantly until jelly thermometer shows temperature of 224°. If no thermometer is used, boil until the jelly sheets off a spoon. Pour immediately into hot sterilized, self-sealing glasses. The jelly is brilliant, light amethyst color. The taste is a tropical treat, slightly salty.

SEAGRAPE JUICE

Place one and a half times as much water as seagrape fruit in a pan and cook until the skin and pulp slips from the stones when the fruit is mashed with a potato masher. Drain the juice off through a jelly bag. Add as much water as pulp and cook 15 minutes more. Drain through jelly bag. If juice is not used for jelly, it may be heated to boiling and then stored in tightly sealed sterilized jars and bottles. If juice is to be used as punch, add half as much sugar as juice, boil a short time, and then bottle and refrigerate.

SEAGRAPE SOUP

Pit 3 cups of ripe seagrapes, and combine with 4 cups of beef consomme. Bring to a boil. Simmer until fruit is tender. Liquify the fruit in a blender and add salt and pepper to taste. Chill and serve in chilled soup cups. If desired, flavor with light rum.

Soursop

This member of the genus *Annona* is a large, dark green, oblong-conical fruit, often irregularly shaped and covered by fleshy recurved spines. The white subacid flesh contains many black seeds. It is seldom cooked and retains its pleasant distinctive taste after being preserved through freezing. Ripe fruit is pureed for freezing by peeling fruit, removing core and seeds and processing through a food mill before packing in freezer containers.

Many of the more than 50 species of the genus *Annona,* native to tropical America, produce edible fruit. The fruits are composed of numerous carpels more or less fused to the fleshy receptacle and exhibit great variation in size and quality. The flesh, white to pinkish, has many dark brown to black seeds imbedded, generally is subacid to sweet with a custardlike consistency. The most popular species are sugar apple, custard apple, soursop, atemoya, rollinia, and cherimoya. They are best eaten freshly picked and chilled but are also used as pulp or juice in drinks, sherbets, and ice creams. These fruits can be used in place of soursop in recipes taking into account the varying sugar content of the various fruits.

SOURSOP CREAM

½ can (14 oz.) sweetened
   condensed milk
1 pt. soursop juice

3 Tbsp. sugar
1 tsp. vanilla
½ tsp. nutmeg

Mix together and chill before serving.

SOURSOP ICE CREAM I

2 cups soursop pulp
1 cup sugar
1 cup milk

1 egg white
1 cup whipping cream

Mix pulp, sugar and milk. Freeze until mushy. Add beaten egg white. Fold in cream which has been beaten. Freeze.

SOURSOP ICE CREAM II

3 whole eggs
1 cup sugar (brown, for
   caramel flavor)
2 cups milk

1 Tbsp. butter
Lemon or vanilla flavoring
2 cups soursop pulp

Mix sugar and eggs. cook with milk and butter in double boiler until thick, stirring occasionally (5 or 10 minutes). Add desired flavoring of lemon or vanilla. Put in refrigerator tray; let freeze until mushy. Stir in 2 cups soursop pulp, which has been run through dilver or a food mill. If wanted extra rich, add 1 cup of heavy whipping cream which has been whipped stiff. Add this with the soursop pulp. Freeze.

SOURSOP MOUSSE

20 marshmallows
½ cup water
2 Tbsp. sugar

1 cup soursop puree
1 cup whipping cream

Add sugar and marshmallows to the water. Place over low heat until a smooth mixture is obtained. When mixture is cool, add soursop puree and let stand in cool place until partially congealed. Add cream which has been whipped. Pour into mold and freeze in refrigerator.

SOURSOP PUNCH

1 medium soursop
Condensed milk to taste

4 glasses water
Pinch salt

Wash and peel soursop. Crush pulp in bowl and gradually add 3 glasses of water, mixing well. Strain. Stir the 4th glass of water into the pulp and mix well. Squeeze and strain again to be sure all flavor is kept. Add salt, milk, and sugar. Serve ice cold.

SOURSOP SHERBET I

¼ cup orange juice
1 qt. milk
1 cup soursop puree

½ cup lemon juice
2½ cups sugar

Combine all ingredients and freeze in a refrigerator tray. When mixture begins to freeze, remove and beat thoroughly. Allow to partially freeze again. Beat a second time. Replace in tray and finish freezing.

SOURSOP SHERBET II

2 cups soursop puree
  (1¾ lb. fruit)
½ cup white corn syrup
2 egg whites
½ cup sugar

½ cup water
1 tsp. unflavored gelatin
½ to ¾ cup sugar
Pinch of salt

Chill corn syrup and egg whites in medium bowl. Sprinkle gelatin over ½ cup of water and let stand 5 minutes; then add ½ cup sugar and salt; heat until dissolved. Cool; add 2 cups soursop puree. Taste, and stir in more sugar if desired. Pour into freezing tray and freeze to mush.

Beat egg white mixture until very stiff. Add frozen soursop mixture and beat until just blended. Pour into 2 freezing trays; moisten bottoms of trays and place on coldest shelf in freezing compartment.

When mixture is frozen stiff (about 1 hour), scrape into chilled bowl; break up with spoon if necessary. Beat until well blended and fluffy. Quickly pile sherbet into trays, return to freezing compartment. Freeze, stirring with a fork once or twice.

SOURSOP SOUFFLE

1 large soursop
3 eggs, separated

Sugar to taste
⅛ tsp. salt

Peel soursop and rub through a sieve or collander, adding water a little at a time. Strain. Heat the juice and sweeten to taste. Beat egg whites until stiff and fold lightly into ¾ cup of heated fruit juice. Add salt. Fill a buttered mold three-fourths full, set in a pan of hot water, and bake in a slow oven until firm. Serve with Sabayon Sauce.

Sabayon Sauce: Beat together 3 egg yolks and 3 Tbsp. powdered sugar. Add 3 Tbsp. sherry. When ready to use, heat in pan over boiling water until the sugar melts and mixture begins to thicken.

SOURSOP TREAT

1 large soursop
4 cups cold water
½ cup rum

½ tsp. grated lime rind
½ tsp. grated nutmeg
Condensed milk to sweeten

Wash and peel soursop. Mash in a bowl with lime rind. Add 2 cups of water. Mix well and strain. Add remainder of water to pulp and strain. Discard pulp and sweeten liquid with milk and add nutmeg. Chill thoroughly. To serve, add rum and pour over cracked ice.

Surinam Cherry

Fruits are about one inch in diameter, deeply ribbed, thin-skinned, and range from light red to almost black. The juicy, sweet, soft, aromatic pulp contains one or two large seeds. The fruit is excellent fresh or in juices, jams, jellies, and pies.

SURINAM CHERRY CAKE

½ cup butter
1½ cups sugar
1½ cups seeded Surinam
    cherries
1 tsp. baking powder
1 tsp. vanilla
1 tsp. soda

2 eggs
2 cups sifted flour
½ tsp. salt
¼ cup buttermilk, sour
    cream or sour milk

Squeeze ½ lime in Surinam cherries. Cream shortening, add sugar gradually, creaming until fluffy. Beat in eggs one at a time. Add seeded Surinam cherries and beat well. Sift together dry ingredients. Add alternately with milk. Add vanilla and blend. Pour in 11½" by 7½" pan and bake 1 hour at 350° or use a tube pan and bake 1½ hours at 350°.

SURINAM CHERRY DRINK

Extract Surinam juice as for jelly (see recipe, p. 158). To 1½ cups of juice add 5 cups of water, juice from 3 limes or 1 cup of orange or grapefruit juice. Sweeten to taste. Pour over crushed ice and serve.

SURINAM CHERRY JAM

3¾ cups seeded Surinam
    cherries
1 cup water

2¾ cups sugar or use 1¾ cups
    sugar and 1 cup mild flavored
    honey

Combine the sugar and water, bring to the boiling point and add cherries. Cook slowly for 20 to 25 minutes until the mixture thickens slightly, but not quite to the jelly test point. Pour into hot, sterile jars and seal immediately.

SURINAM CHERRY JELLY

5 lb. Surinam cherries
7½ cups water or enough to
  barely cover fruit

1 cup sugar to each cup of
  juice

Wash cherries, remove stems and blossom ends. Add water to the fruit and simmer for 25 minutes, or until the cherries are soft. Strain the juice through a flannel jelly bag. Measure the juice and place it in a shallow kettle with a capacity at least four times the volume of juice.

Heat to the boiling point and boil 5 minutes. Add the sugar and remove the scum as the mixture starts to boil. Boil rapidly until the juice gives the jelly test (sheets off the spoon in large drops). Pour the jelly into hot, sterile glasses and seal immediately.

SURINAM CHERRY PIE

1½ cups seeded Surinam
  cherries
½ cup seedless raisins
¾ cup diced apple

1 cup sugar
3 Tbsp. flour
1 Tbsp. butter
Unbaked double pie shell

Line a pie tin with pastry. Mix the fruit and pour into the pie shell. Sprinkle with flour and sugar and dot with small pieces of butter. Moisten the edge of the pie crust and cover with a second crust. Place in a hot over (450°) for 10 minutes, then reduce the temperature to 350° and bake for 30 to 40 minutes or until the fruit is soft.

SURINAM RELISH

3 oranges
1 qt. seeded Surinam cherries
1 cup sugar
1 cup water

2 cups chopped celery
½ cup vinegar
1 tsp. salt

Peel oranges, saving the rind of one orange, grind this through the food chopper and add the chopped flesh of the other oranges. Add the cherries and celery. Make a syrup of the sugar, water, vinegar, and salt. Add to fruit mixture and boil 2 minutes. Put in jars and seal. Process 15 minutes in boiling water.

Tamarind

The ripe fruit is a brittle, brown pod, two to six inches long. When green and very acid it can be used to season fish and meat. When mature, the pod contains several large seeds surrounded by brown, pasty, tart, datelike pulp which is the part usually used in recipes.

FRESH TAMARINDADE

21 shelled tamarinds	¾ cup sugar
6 cups water	

Add tamarinds to water and let stand 10 hours. Stir well, strain. Add sugar and chill. Serve with cracked ice.

PHILIPPINE TAMARIND CHUTNEY

1 lb. dates	¼ lb. brown sugar
½ lb. green ginger root	2 Tbsp. salt
1 lb. Malaga raisins	1 cup tarragon vinegar
1 lb. onions	½ lb. tamarinds
¼ lb. chili peppers	

Shell tamarinds. Remove seeds from tamarinds, dates, and raisins. Chop the fruit together. Chop onions and chilies. Scrape and slice ginger root. Combine all ingredients. Seal in sterile jars.

PRESERVED TAMARINDS

Remove the crisp brown shells from the tamarinds and pack the pulp with the seeds in a firm layer in a sterilized jar. Add equal layers of brown sugar, until jar is filled. Seal and store in a cool dark place for at least three months before using.

TAMARINDADE

1 cup tamarind syrup	6 sprigs of mint
4¾ cups water	

Mix syrup (see recipe, page 161) and water. Chill and serve with cracked ice. Place a sprig of mint in each glass.

TAMARIND BUTTER

Remove shells from tamarinds, cover pulp and seeds with water, and let stand overnight. The next morning simmer slowly until seeds can be removed. This pulp can be combined with mango, Malay apple, guava, or similar fruit. Add sugar to taste and cook to desired consistency.

TAMARIND GUAVA CHUTNEY

3 lb. prepared guavas	3 lb. tamarinds
3 lb. brown sugar	3 pods chili pepper, dried
2 lb. raisins	2 cloves garlic
1 pt. pimiento	I lb. onions
I lb. green ginger	¼ cup white mustard seed
1 Tbsp. each: ground allspice,	¼ cup celery seed
cloves, cinnamon, salt	¼ Tbsp. pepper
	2 qt. vinegar

Remove shells from tamarinds and soak pulp in vinegar, stirring often to remove the pulp from the seed. When the pulp is softened, press fruit through a colander. Put guavas, from which seeds have been removed, through medium knife of food chopper. Put raisins through the same chopper. Use the finest blade for the ginger, peppers, garlic, onions, and mustard seed. Boil ingredients together 30 minutes. Let stand overnight. Reheat to boiling point and pour into sterilized jars.

TAMARIND ICE

1 cup tamarind pulp	1¾ cups water
1 cup sugar	1 Tbsp. gelatin

Boil water and sugar for five minutes. Soak the gelatin in 3 Tbsp. cold water. Add to the hot syrup. Cool and add tamarind pulp. Freeze until firm. Put in a mixer bowl and beat until fluffy. Return to freezer.

TAMARIND SYRUP

2 cups tamarind pulp	5 cups sugar
6 cups water	

To prepare pulp, pour water over shelled tamarinds and allow to stand overnight. Add sugar and boil 20 minutes. Strain through a coarse sieve, pressing pulp through. Heat syrup to boiling point. Pour into sterilized jars and seal. This syrup can be used in curry, chutneys, or drinks.

White Sapote

These ovoid fruits reach 3 inches in diameter and have a thin green skin which turns greenish-yellow at maturity. The creamy or yellowish flesh, juicy and of melting texture, has a distinctive sweet flavor. Fruits have one to five large ellipsoid seeds. If picked mature and firm they will soften to edible state in a couple of days. Although the white sapote may be preferred by many as a dessert fruit with cream and sugar, it is a delicious substitute for other tropical fruits in many recipes.

WHITE SAPOTE BREAD

1¾ cups flour, sifted
2¾ tsp. baking powder
½ tsp. salt
⅓ cup shortening

⅔ cup sugar
2 eggs
1 cup mashed sapote

Sift together flour, baking powder, and salt. Beat shortening in mixing bowl until creamy. Add sugar and eggs. Continue beating at medium speed 1 minute. Add white sapote to egg mixture. Mix until blended. Add flour mixture, beating at low speed for 30 seconds. Do not over-beat. Turn into greased loaf pan and bake at 350° about one hour.

WHITE SAPOTE SALAD

Chill, then peel white sapotes. Cut into chips or suitable pieces. For each cup of the fruit use a cup of cottage cheese, mix lightly. Chill. If desired use a dressing made of 1 Tbsp. of lemon juice and 2 Tbsp. of mayonnaise. Serve on lettuce leaf. Garnish with halves of Surinam cherry.

WHITE SAPOTE SAUCE

Prepare white sapotes by peeling and cutting fruit into slices. Cook slightly over medium heat and mash if desired. Season to taste with sugar and lemon juice. Can be frozen or eaten in place of applesauce; also delicious over ice cream.

CALORIES AND VITAMIN INFORMATION

	CALORIES per pound	VITAMINS A Caro-tene	B-1 Thia-mine	B-2 Ribo-flavin	B-3 Niacin	C
Akee	*	*	*	*	*	*
Antidesma	*	P	P	E	F	*
Avocado	128	F	F	G	G	P
Banana	85	F	P	F	F	F
Barbados Cherry	28	F	P	P	P	E
Black Sapote	*	P	O	P	P	E
Breadfruit	103	P	G	F	G	F
Calamondin	*	G	G	P	P	G
Canistel	80	P	P	P	G	G
Carambola	25	P	P	P	F	G
Carissa	70	P	P	F	P	E
Coconut	346	O	P	P	F	O
Dovyalis	*	F	P	F	P	E
Fig	80	P	P	P	P	P
Grumichama	*	P	P	P	P	F
Guava	62	P	P	P	F	E
Jaboticaba	*	*	*	*	*	E
Jakfruit	576	*	P	P	P	F
Jambolan	*	O	P	E	P	E
Kumquat	65	E	E	E	*	E
Lime	18	O	P	P	P	E
Loquat	48	E	P	P	P	P
Longan/Lychee	64	O	P	F	F	E
Macadamia	691	*	G	G	G	*
Malay Apple	*	*	*	*	*	*
Mamey Sapote	*	P	P	P	F	F
Mango	66	E	P	F	F	E
Mysore Raspberry	73	P	G	E	P	E
Papaya	39	E	P	F	P	E
Passion Fruit	90`	G	P	G	G	G
Persimmon	77	G	G	F	F	E
Pineapple	52	P	G	P	P	P
Plantain	119	F	P	F	F	F
Roselle	*	F	P	P	P	F
Sapodilla	80	F	P	P	P	E
Soursop	65	O	F	G	G	F
Surinam Cherry	51	G	P	P	E	F
Tamarind	239	O	G	E	G	P
White Sapote	*	*	*	*	*	*

* Data unobtained

E - Excellent   G - Good   F - Fair   P - Poor   O - None

FREEZING FLORIDA FRUITS

What does freezing do?

Freezing preserves food by stopping the growth of bacteria, molds, and yeasts and retards the activity of enzymes. It does not destroy micro-organisms or enzymes.

How long will frozen foods keep?

The length of time frozen foods hold their fresh flavor and color depends on the kind and freshness of food used, its selection and preparation, whether freezing wrap or container is air tight, and the temperature of the freezing unit.

How much food will freeze at a time?

Prepare food for freezing as soon as possible after picking. The food should be cold when it is packed. Speed in the freezing process is important to maintain quality. Only the amount of food that will freeze in a 24-hour period should be put into the freezer at one time. Approximately 2-3 pounds per cubic foot of freezer space is the amount to prepare during one 24-hour period.

Why is 0° F. necessary?

Frozen food held at 0° F., or lower, retains quality longer than foods stored at a higher temperature. When the temperature is above 0° F., the loss in quality speeds up even though food remains cold and hard.

What kind of containers are recommended?

Packaging materials should be moisture-proof and durable. Most containers made especially for freezing are suitable. Glass canning jars may be used for fruits if enough headspace (space between food and closure) is left for the food to expand. Heavy aluminum foil and strong plastic containers protect food from freezer burn; but ordinary wax paper and flimsy wax-lined cartons are seldom strong enough or moisture-proof.

What is the best way to pack food?

Pack cold food tightly into containers. Since most foods expand after freezing, allow ample headspace. The amount of space will vary, depending on food and size of containers. When packing food in bags, press excess air from the bag before sealing. Label and date each package.

FREEZING DIRECTIONS

Selection and Preparation

Select firm, ripe fruit: firmness for texture; ripeness for flavor. Wash all fruit in cold water, lifting the fruit out of the water so that dirt and trash are left in the water. Drain the fruit. Never leave it soaking in water. Finish preparing and immediately pack it into containers.

Packing Fruit

Fruit may be packed successfully in one of three ways: syrup pack, sugar pack, and unsweetened pack. Most fruits retain better texture, color, and flavor if packed in syrup or sugar. Mild-flavored fruits, such as loquat, figs, and melons, need only a 30% syrup but the majority of fruits require a 40% solution. A 50% syrup is recommended for blueberries, Surinam cherries, and strawberries. Extra sour fruits, such as some varieties of cherries, do well in a 60% syrup.

Table for Syrup

	Sugar (cups)	Water (cups)	Yield (cups)
30% syrup	2	4	5
40% syrup	3	4	5½
50% syrup	4¾	4	6½
60% syrup	7	4	7¾

Sugar Pack

Mix sugar with fruit until the sugar is dissolved. Pack into containers and place a small piece of crumpled water-resistant paper on top to hold the fruit under the juice.

Unsweetened Pack

Pack prepared fruits plain without the addition of syrup or sugar. Some fruits may be sliced and frozen individually in a tray before packing.

Prevent Darkening

Light-colored fruits have a tendency to turn dark when exposed to air. To prevent discoloration, these fruits may be pre-treated by one of the following methods:

Ascorbic Acid Ascorbic acid (vitamin C) is very effective in preserving color. Directions for use are generally given on the package.

Citric Acid Citric acid in crystallizing or powdered form is available at most drug stores. Follow directions recommended for the specific fruit.

Sugar Syrup Sugar syrup tends to prevent discoloration by excluding air. Slice fruit directly into the syrup and use the syrup for packing.

Salt Solution To prevent light fruit from darkening during preparation, slice fruit into a salt solution containing two tablespoons salt to one gallon of water. Leave the fruit in the solution no longer than 20 minutes; drain it before packing.

Packing Points

Syrup Pack Cover fruit with syrup; leave ½-inch headspace for pints and 1 inch for quarts.

Sugar Pack Mix fruit with sugar until the sugar is dissolved and syrup is formed. Leave ½-inch headspace for pints; 1 inch for quarts.

Unsweetened Pack (dry pack) Leave ½-inch headspace.

Recommended Storage Periods for Fruits (for optimum flavor)

Freezer 0° F.

Most home-frozen fruits	8-12 months
Home-frozen citrus fruits	4-6 months

Some Freezing Terms

Blanch (scald) To heat fruits in boiling water or steam in order to slow or stop the action of enzymes.

Enzymes Naturally occurring substances that help promote organic change (ripening, decomposition, etc.) in vegetable or animal tissues. Their action must be stopped before certain food is frozen in order to prevent loss of quality, flavor, and color.

Freezer burn Dehydration of improperly wrapped food, leading to loss of color, flavor, and texture.

Headroom Space left at top of container to allow for expansion of food as it freezes.

FRUIT LEATHER

Leather is dried fruit puree. It is often spiked with chopped nuts, finely ground citrus rinds and seasonings such as cinnamon, nutmeg, coriander, allspice, etc. It can be sweetened with honey, sugar, molasses, raisins, dates, or figs. Flavor can be adjusted with vanilla, almond or lemon extract. Due to their high pectin content, apples combine well with many tropical fruits for preparing leather. The flavor and sweetness of the puree can be adjusted easily to taste in the liquid stage.

To make leather, prepare the fruit as for cooking. Cut up into the blender, adding only as much water as required to liquify the fruit. Juicy fruits such as berries, mangos, guavas, require no extra liquid. Consistency should be that of thick apple sauce, runny but definitely not a liquid. The runnier it is, the longer it will take to dry and the stickier it will be. Do not add nuts while the fruit is in the blender as they will be ground too fine.

The leather is dried in trays lined with plastic wrap or non-stick trays. If plastic wrap is used it should be fastened to the outside of the tray to prevent covering the edge of the leather and so prevent the edge from drying properly.

Pour about ½ inch into a tray and place in the dryer. If done in an oven, the top should be dry in 24 hours at 110°. The leather may need turning and drying on the other side until it has a sticky surface and appears translucent.

Leather can be rolled up and stored in cool, dark, airtight containers. It should be kept in the dark and will last easily for a year if refrigerated. Leather is a wonderful snack and an intelligent method of utilizing excess fruit. Try any combination. Do not add chopped dates until after blending or thin crunchiness will be lost. Berries are too juicy alone. Blend them, strain out seeds, add apples, and sweeten if desired.

FRUIT WINES

Wine can be made from any fruit. There are many books on wine making and many recipes, so only a few points on the process and one recipe that can be adjusted for most fruits are presented. There are certain basic procedures, materials, and cautions which help to produce an acceptable product. The most important are presented below.

Fermentation Vessel: Use a glass, ceramic, plastic or stainless steel vessel, large enough to prevent foam-over during fermentation. It is best for the capacity to be twice the quantity to be fermented.

Cleanliness: If everything is not scrupulously clean, poor quality wine or even vinegar will be the product. After all equipment to be used has been washed in hot water and soap and then rinsed well, it should be sterilized with a solution of sodium bisulphite (2 Tbsp. per cup of water).

Yeast: Wine yeast should be used as it is bred to live in alcohol. Bakers yeast or no yeast may work but vinegar often results.

Yeast Nutrients: Yeast nutrients should be used to provide favorable condition for the yeast to do its work.

Fruit Acids: Good wine requires proper balance between acid and sugar. Some fruits are not high enough in acid; hence, the addition of a blend of malic and citric acids is required.

Pectic Enzyme: Addition of pectic enzyme causes the finely divided fruit particles, which cloud the wine, to settle out.

Sugar: Most fruits require sugar. Two pounds per gallon of liquid is the average amount which, when fermented out, will produce a dry wine. If desired, the wine can then be sweetened with the syrup made of 2 parts sugar to one of water.

Hydrometer: This instrument is very helpful in wine making. The amount of sugar in the "must" and hence the potential alcohol content of the wine meter. Reference should be made to a book on wine making for more detailed explanation of the use of a hydrometer.

Racking: A considerable amount of fine sediment (lees) will settle out of the wine. The removal of the clear liquid above this sediment is called racking. It is done by siphoning so as to not disturb the sediment. The pectic enzymes aid the settling of the lees. It may be necessary to rack the wine several times before bottling.

Secondary Fermenter: This is a glass, ceramic, plastic, or stainless steel vessel into which the wine is racked after the primary fermentation has tapered off. It should be provided with an air lock to allow the carbon dioxide to escape but prevent air from entering to bring in undesirable oxygen, bacteria, or wild yeasts.

FRUIT WINE RECIPE

The recipe below can be used for many fruits. It is written for one gallon and can be used for larger quantities by appropriately multiplying the quantities; no increase in yeast is required.

Fruit — 3½ lb. before peeling
  or pitting
Water — to make 1 gallon
White sugar — 2 lb. (hydrometer
  to read 1.085 to 1.100 for dry)
Grape tannin — ¼ tsp.
Acid blend — 1 Tbsp.

Pectic enzyme — ½ tsp.
Wine yeast — 1 packet
Yeast nutrient — 1 tablet
Sterilizer — 1 tsp. solution
  (2 Tbsp. sodium bisulphite
  per 1 cup water)

Peel and pit fruit, mash into sterilized pail with some water, add 1 Tbsp. sterilizing solution. Cover pail to leave overnight. This will kill wild yeasts and bacteria, thus saving the product from becoming vinegar. Next day add other ingredients to primary fermenter and leave 7-10 days well covered. Then strain out the "must" and put wine into secondary fermenter with air lock, rack off as desired. It should clear in one to two months, then bottle. Sweeten to taste and add 1 ascorbic acid tablet per gallon as an anti-oxidant, and 1 tsp. sterilizing solution per gallon to prevent refermentation. Wines are generally better if aged 1-2 years.

Many stores carry wine-making supplies and will have all of those discussed above.

JELLY MAKING

Home cooked jellies made with home grown fruits far surpass in flavor those sold in the market. Jelly is made by cooking fruit juice with sugar until the jell stage is reached. The jelly should be clear and firm so that it will retain its shape when cut. Fruit suited to making jelly needs to have both pectin and acid. A mixture of ripe fruit for color and flavor and slightly underripe for its pectin may be used. Pectin, like starch, is a carbohydrate and is found just under the fruit's skin. Cooking the fruit extracts the pectin.

Fruit that has a strong acid or tart taste is usually acid enough. If the taste is subacid, add lemon/lime juice to acidify the juice. To compare the pectin content, compare the taste with a mixture of one teaspoon lemon juice, three tablespoons water, and one-half teaspoon sugar.

To extract the fruit juice for jelly, cut off stems and blossom ends and cut up fruit, retaining seeds and cores. Cook in very little water until soft, 5 to 20 minutes. Strain through cheesecloth but do not squeeze or jelly will be cloudy. Then strain the juice through a flannel jelly bag. Jelly may be made immediately or the juice may be stored until later use.

Certain steps must be followed to prepare superior jelly.

1. Use a large flat-bottomed enamel or aluminum pan.

2. Use no more than 4 cups of juice at a time.

3. Measure juice and sugar accurately.

4. Boil juice 2-3 minutes to evaporate some of the liquid before adding sugar.

5. Add sugar gradually to boiling juice.

6. If commercial pectin is used, follow the package instructions.

7. With jelly thermometer, boil to 220°F. Otherwise check with sheet test. Dip a large spoon into liquid and lift spoon so drops fall off the edge. When the drops run together into a sheet, remove from fire.

8. During the jelly boiling period wash jelly glasses and boil at least 10 minutes to sterilize.

9. Skim and pour jelly immediately into hot glasses. Fill to ½ inch of the top and wipe edge of glass to remove all trace of jelly. Put on metal lid and screw down metal band. Invert jars for a minute so the hot liquid will sterilize the lids. Cool on a rack, label, and store in a dark place.

Pastries

GLAZE FOR TARTS

Mix ¾ cup of any fruit juice with 1 tablespoon of cornstarch. Place in top of double boiler and add 2 tablespoons of sugar. Stir constantly until liquid is thick. Cool slightly and pour over the tarts.

SWEDISH PANCAKES

1 cup flour	3 eggs
2 Tbsp. sugar	3 cups milk
¼ tsp. salt	2 Tbsp. melted butter

Sift flour. Add sugar and salt. Stir in eggs and milk gradually. Add butter. Pour batter by tablespoonfuls into hot buttered pan and brown both sides. Place on hot platter and serve with berries or jam. Serves 4.

Pancakes may be made in 7 inch frying pan and folded in half, placing fruits or jams in the center. Place in chafing dish that has been buttered and serve with fruit juice spooned over the top.

TART SHELLS

2 cups flour	1 cup butter
2 egg yolks	Grated rind of 1 lemon
2 Tbsp. sugar	Pinch of salt

Place 2 cups of flour on pastry board and in a well in the center add the 2 egg yolks, sugar, butter, lemon, and salt. Mix these ingredients to a smooth paste and work in the flour, adding a little ice water, if necessary, to moisten the dough. It is not easy to roll this dough, so press lightly with the fingers ½ inch thick into a buttered shallow pan or onto a baking sheet. Chill in the refrigerator for 30 minutes.

Cut rounds of dough to fit the tart pans and prick with a fork to prevent bubbling. Bake in hot over (450°) until delicately browned.

FILLINGS FOR TARTS

Baked individual tart shells may be filled with sweetened fresh fruit or well-drained cooked fruit. The fruit may be mixed with whipped cream, custard, or cream cheese sweetened and softened with milk and whipped until fluffy.

Index

173